Brain-friendly Learning

A Powerful Handbook for Teenagers

By Ron Fitzgerald, D.Ed.

Author: Ronald Fitzgerald

26 Forest Rd.

Acton, MA 01720

This edition published by

Dog Ear Publishing

4010 W. 86th Street, Ste H

Indianapolis, IN 46268

www.dogearpublishing.net

ISBN: 978-160844-298-0

This book is printed on acid-free paper.

Printed in the United States of America

Table of Contents

Table of Contents

List of Figures

List of Tables

Dedication

This handbook is dedicated in honor of:

- Sebastian Paquette - - a teacher who managed the most brain-friendly classroom I have ever seen.
- Eric Jensen - - a dedicated scholar, prolific author, and international consultant who with the help of his wife Diane has shown thousands of educators the value of brain-friendly teaching and learning.
- All of the talented teachers and students with whom I have been fortunate to work and who used, enjoyed, and demonstrated the great power of brain-friendly learning.

Preface

This compact handbook has one purpose - - to help any high school or middle school student to gain more learning, thinking, and career power by using recent brain research. Each brain is unique. This handbook will help the reader to discover how his or her unique brain works best and how to use it most effectively.

Most pages are arranged in brain-friendly sets - - a graphic or summary images on the left page and related text on the right page of each set. You can use the graphics for a preview or for a quick review of each chapter.

While some schools use the handbook as part of a program on HOW TO LEARN. Others use it to provide teachers with a reference for converting traditional teaching techniques into more brain-friendly techniques. However, the primary use of the handbook is for self-study by teenagers who want to invest in the power of improved learning. You can easily study one brief chapter in each of four sequential weekend sessions as a great investment in your personal future. Have fun sharpening your brain power!

Brain-friendly Learning

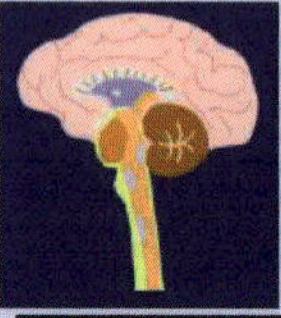

Does brain-friendly learning work better?

- Many elementary schools have doubled test scores with brain-friendly teaching.
- Many companies and the U.S. Army have more than halved learning time by using this type of learning.
- In Minuteman Regional High school in Massachusetts, many reading lab students gained 3 to 4 years in reading skills tests in one school year.

FIGURE # 1

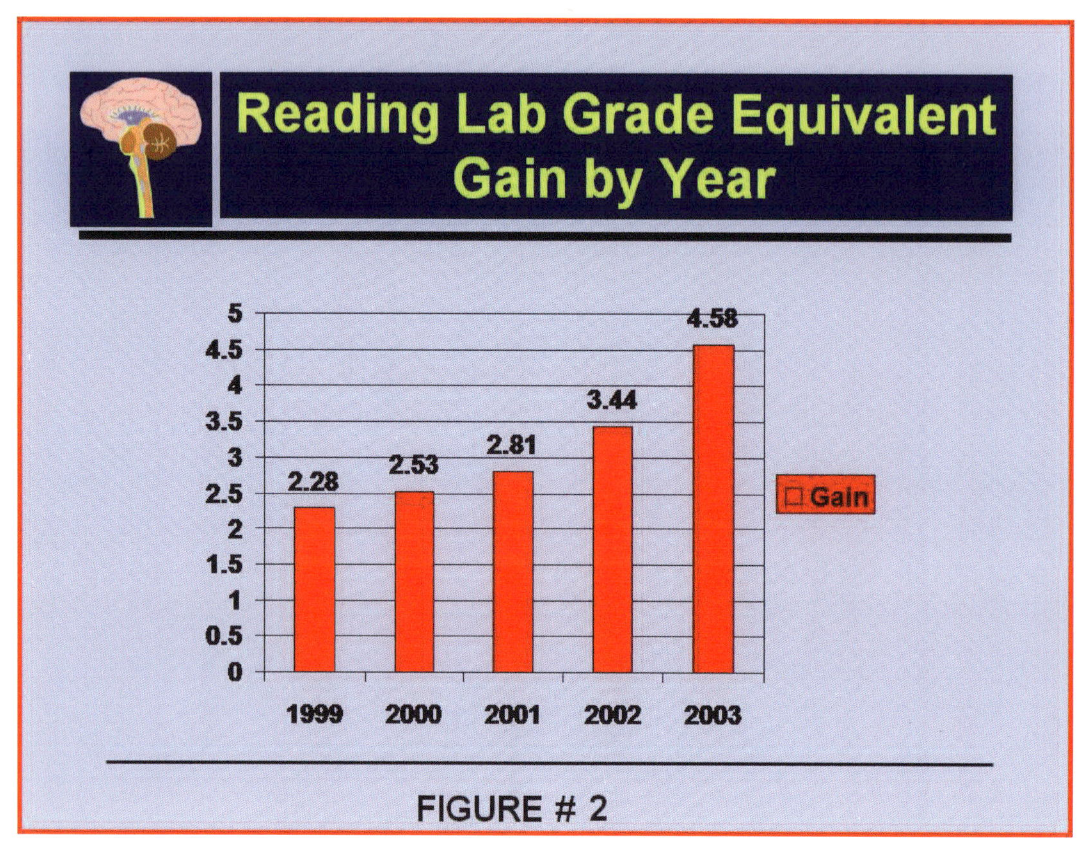

FIGURE # 2

CHAPTER 1

Introduction: Why Use Brain-friendly Learning?

In the past twenty years, more has been discovered about how the brain works than in previous recorded history. We now know that different people learn best in different ways. Using the ways that work best for you is called brain-friendly learning. You should use this approach because it works much better than the traditional approach of everyone being expected to learn in exactly the same way. It helps you to increase your learning as an investment in your future.

Look at Figure #1 on the page to the left. It lists three examples from types of organizations that have helped their students or employees use brain-friendly learning techniques. The first item in Figure #1 refers to elementary schools like one in Greensboro, N.C., where test scores doubled after use of brain-friendly teaching and learning techniques. The second item refers to adult learners with whom brain-friendly learning is often called "accelerated learning" because companies like Bell Atlantic, Chevron, Commonwealth Edison, and others have halved learning time using the learning techniques. They have often achieved much higher results at the same time. Brain-friendly learning works with all ages. The third item refers to high school results which we shall look at in more detail. Study Figure #2.

In Minuteman Regional High School, some students entering grade nine did not have reading skill levels strong enough to profit fully from technical majors that they elected. We enrolled those students in a computer-based reading lab that let each student learn in his or her best way for one year. Some needed programs with a strong auditory or hearing focus. Some others needed lots of visual help to accelerate their reading skills. The lab software gave them learning options and constantly measured their progress. As shown in Figure #2, in the first year of lab operation students averaged a 2.28 year gain in reading skill, over double the learning growth rate in traditional school progress. With each school year, the teachers introduced more and more brain-friendly or accelerated techniques. By the fifth school year of lab operation, students in the one-year classes were averaging over four years of reading skill growth in one school year! This same sort of accelerated progress was being achieved by students in some other classes in the school; we shall consider another Minuteman example in a moment.

For now, be aware of this reality. Learning traditional school subjects - - mathematics, science, English, etc. – is important. However for your own sake, never neglect this very important subject - - LEARNING HOW TO LEARN. Some schools do not do enough in this area. This booklet can help you to help yourself in developing the brain-friendly learning techniques that are so powerful.

In a second Minuteman example, teacher Sebastian Paquette taught a class called English for the Entrepreneur. It used projects like the preparation of a business plan and a business lease to teach English skills. Mr. Paquette introduced more and more brain-friendly learning techniques to students every year. He taught the students about different ways of learning. He had them practice the different learning techniques. He presented material in different ways, not depending too heavily on lectures and reading. He gave students some learning choices and accepted the fact that some needed more time or help on certain tasks than others needed. While doing this, he used the same objective standards to evaluate the quality of projects completed from year to year. Theoretically, if brain-friendly learning helped, student scores on projects should improve every year. They did! Figure #3 on the next page shows year to year progress on a business lease project.

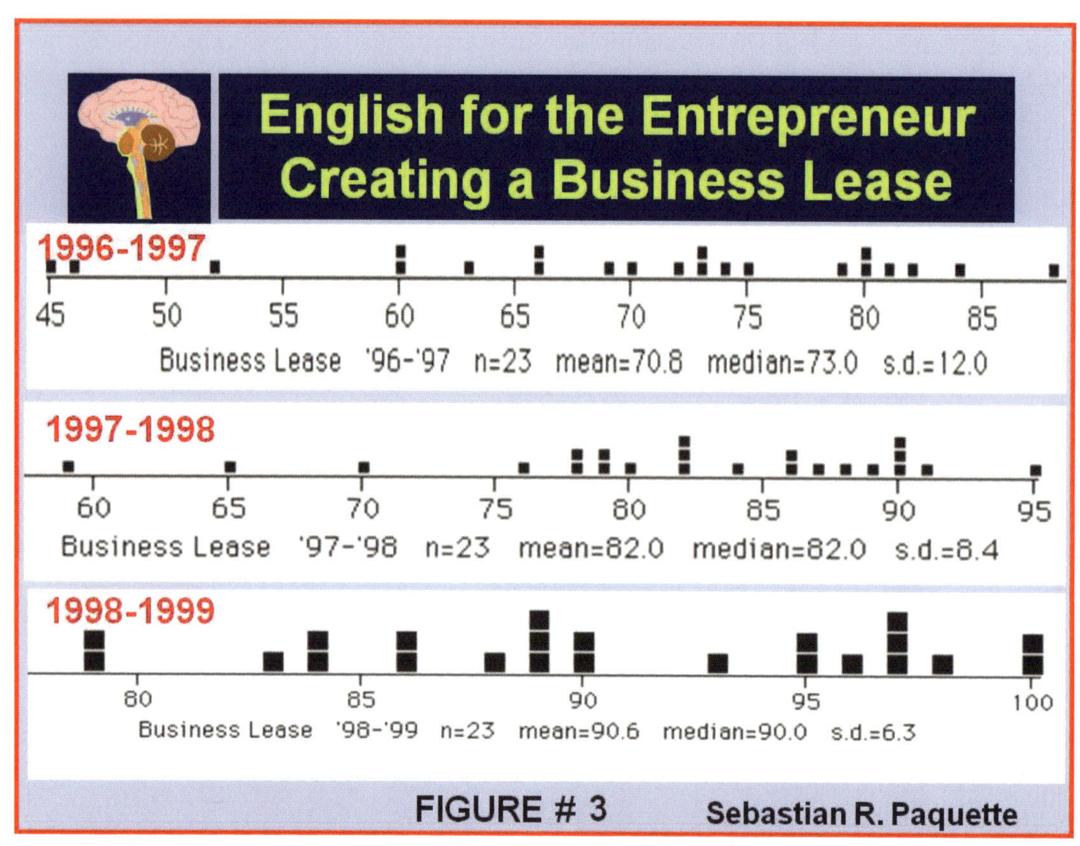

FIGURE # 3

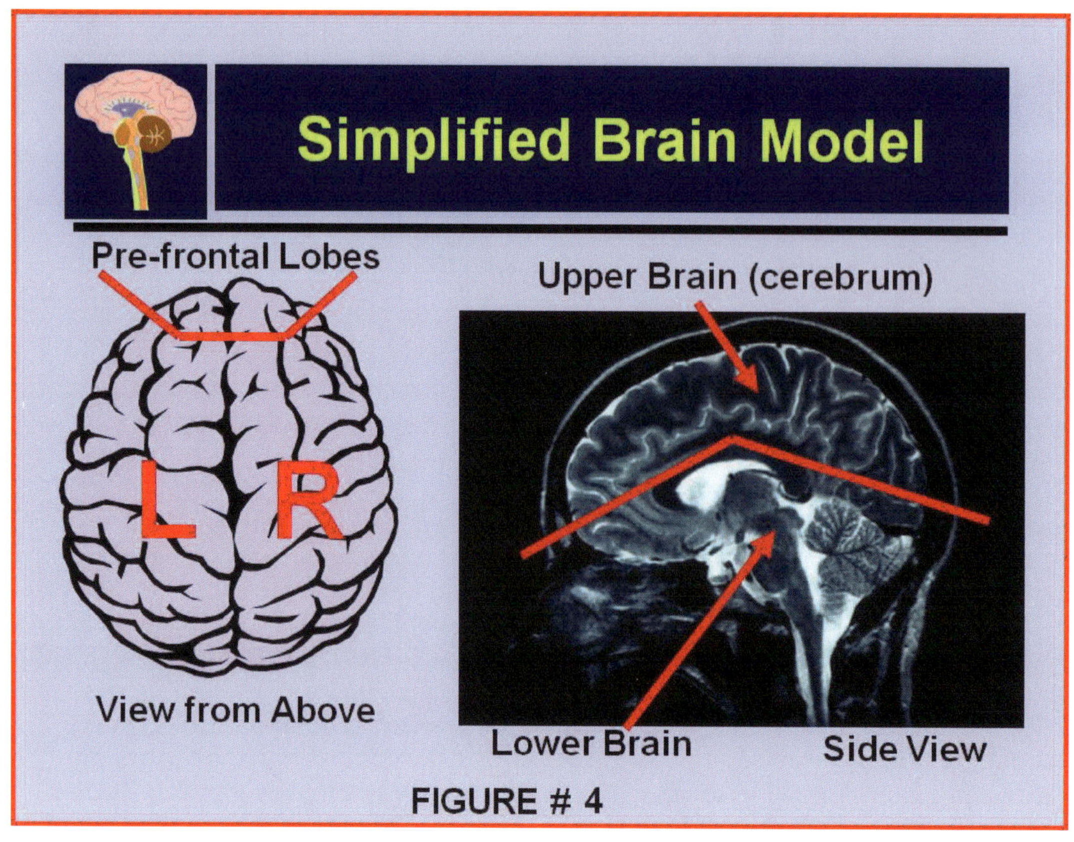

FIGURE # 4

In Figure #3, each small square on the yearly charts represents a student score. In the 1996-97 school year, the average or mean grade on the business lease project was 70.8; the lowest grade was 45. By the 1998-99 school year, the average or mean grade on this project using the same evaluation standards was 90.6 and the lowest grade was 79. Increased use of brain-friendly techniques led to increased learning. Students became very proud of their learning and viewed the experience of being in Mr. Paquette's class as both fun and life-changing. Like students in Mr. Paquette's classes, you can enjoy the fun and the power of accelerated learning techniques and even share them with others.

Before we begin looking at specific techniques you might use, let us look at a brain model or diagrams that can help you to understand two different ways of looking at the brain. Consider Figure #4 on the page to the left. The picture on the left side of the figure shows that the brain has a left half or hemisphere which I have marked L and right half or hemisphere which I have marked R. The two sides of the brain are connected by a large bundle of nerves called the corpus callosum; so both halves work together rather than separately. Yet each half tends to focus on the world a little differently. Some people favor a left-brain focus; others favor a right-brain focus. Also notice the label on the front part of the brain - - the pre-frontal lobes. On the last page of chapter 3, we shall describe the importance of the pre-frontal lobes.

The side view picture on the right side of Figure #4 emphasizes that there is an upper brain or cerebrum and a lower brain. The upper and lower parts again tend to address different functions but also work together. In chapter 3, we review the importance of the upper brain and lower brain functions combined with the left and right functions - - a four part model.

Chapter 4 will review a brain preference test that you can use to analyze YOUR brain in relation to our four-part model - - left, right, upper, and lower. The emphasis will be on using test results to use your brain most effectively because no two brains are exactly the same.

Review Questions for Chapter 1

Which of these four statements is true? Answers can be found in the Appendix.

1. Different people learn best in different ways.
2. Brain-friendly learning techniques helped some high school students grow as much as three or four years in reading skill level in one school year.
3. A large nerve bundle connects the left brain and right brain.
4. You can use a brain test to analyze your left, right, upper, and lower brain functions.

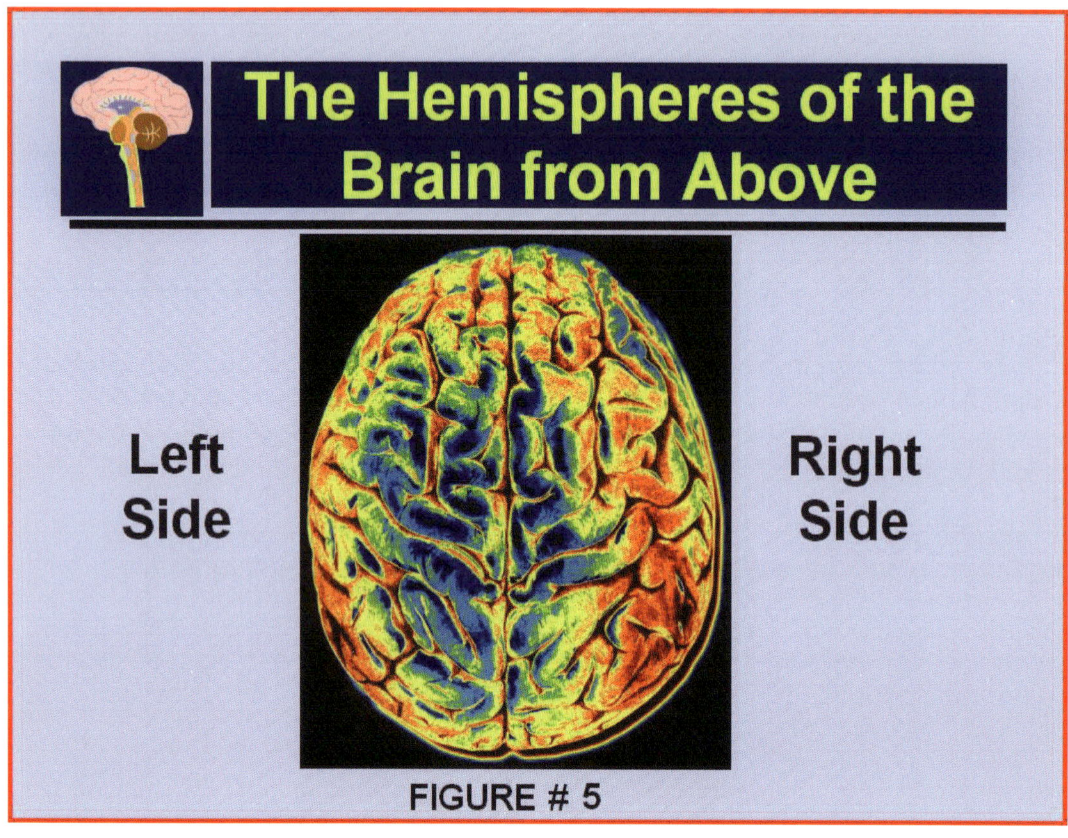

FIGURE # 5

Take a brain quiz now to discover which side of your brain is more dominant. Go to this internet site:

http://homeworktips.about.com/od/learningstyles/a/brainquiz.htm

Click on "TAKE THE QUIZ." If this does not bring you to a quiz, use Google to search for "left brain right brain quiz" to see a number of choices from which you can select one.

Chapter 2

Receiving Information

Receiving information is a first step in learning. Figure #5 on the page to the left reminds you again that the brain has a left side or hemisphere and a right side. Each side tends to receive and process information differently. Although we all use both sides, many of us have a more dominant side. Being conscious of any dominance can help you to know how to learn more effectively.

The web site references under Figure #5 can lead you to a place where you can take a simple quiz to discover any dominance or preferences in your brain operation. I suggest that you take such a quiz before continuing to read this chapter.

TABLE #1 below shows common characteristics of left and right dominance:

TABLE #1: LEFT BRAIN AND RIGHT BRAIN CHARACTERISTICS

Left Brain Characteristics	**Right Brain Characteristics**
1. Uses logic.	1. Uses intuition and imagination.
2. Likes step by step order.	2. Likes randomness.
3. Enjoys words and numbers.	3. Prefers images and pictures.
4. Focuses on details.	4. Focuses on the big picture.
5. Prefers working alone or leading.	5. Prefers working with others.
6. Is deliberate.	6. Is spontaneous.
7. Can listen to lectures.	7. Gets bored with lectures.

Keep in mind that very few people are totally left dominant or right dominant. For example on brain preference tests, this author is 66% left dominant and 34% right dominant. I like logic and order and make "to do" lists. However, I greatly prefer learning from images and charts and doing things rather than just listening or reading. In fact, many people on both sides of the dominance scale profit greatly from visual and hands-on learning. So, use the results of brain preference tests very carefully. Realize that you probably have characteristics from both types of dominance. Adjust your learning methods accordingly.

Begin now to get to know YOUR brain a little better. Copy TABLE #2 from the next page on a separate sheet of paper. In the left half of that copy, list what you believe are your top five characteristics from TABLE #1, placing an L for left or an R for right before each one. In the right half of your copy of TABLE #2, place the top five items of learning advice that appeal to you from the two lists that begin below and continue on the next page. Again, place an L or an R before each item. You will then have an initial self-analysis of your brain preferences. You can refine this list as you continue reading in this booklet.

Here is a list of learning advice related to the earlier list of characteristics of left brain dominance in TABLE #1:

1. Review and use the auditory learning style covered later in this chapter.

TABLE 2: MY BRAIN PREFERENCES

My Preferred Characteristics from Table #1	**Learning Advice I prefer from Lists on Page 8.**
1.	1.
2.	2.
3.	3.
4.	4.
5.	5.

2. Do homework in a quiet place. Talk and even music might distract you.

3. Plan your study schedule and follow the plan.

4. Take good notes and make an outline. Use them to study for tests.

5. Consider using your strengths to take challenging math and science courses.

6. Be a leader in group activities at school, but study alone.

7. When teachers give you choices for learning or demonstrating learning, select the option that uses your preference strengths.

8. Look over the following advice related to the list of right brain dominance. Do any of the items appeal to you? Even if they do not appeal to you, practice some right brain skills in your spare time. This will strengthen your whole brain capability and give you more flexibility for dealing with different types of learning tasks

Using what works best for you will help you to increase your learning efficiency.

Here is a list of learning advice related to the characteristics list of right brain dominance in TABLE #1:

1. Review and use the visual learning style covered later in this chapter. Also consider the somatic learning style which might apply to you.

2. Seek images, videos, and charts to help you study. Teachers and parents can work with you to get visual materials on subjects like math and science.

3. Force yourself to plan and use a well organized study schedule. Do not lose it or forget about it as you might tend to do.

4. Use simple pictures and meaningful doodles in the notes you take in class or while reading. The images or pictures will work better for you than words alone.

5. Use your imagination and natural creativity in writing English essays. Focus on the people aspects of history.

6. Enjoy working and even studying with others.

7. Preview assigned books or chapters by reading the table of contents and/or chapter headings. This gives you the big picture before details. Thank teachers who give you an advance overview of a course and individual units.

8. When teachers give you choices for learning or demonstrating learning, select the option that uses your preference strengths.

9. Look over the previous advice related to the list of left brain dominance. Do any of the items appeal to you? Even if they do not appeal to you, practice some left brain skills in your spare time. This will strengthen your whole brain capability and give you more flexibility for dealing with different types of learning tasks.

10. When and if you have a choice of teachers or schools or colleges, gather information and consider selecting those known for paying attention to different learning styles by

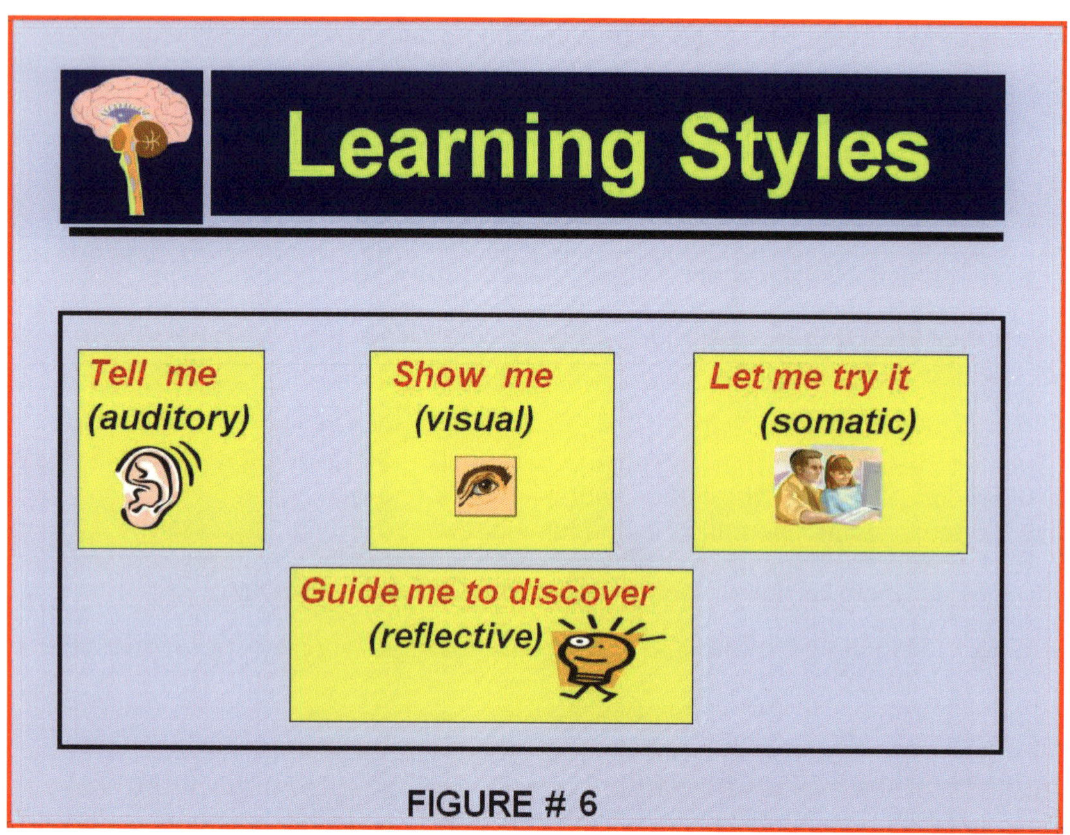

FIGURE # 6

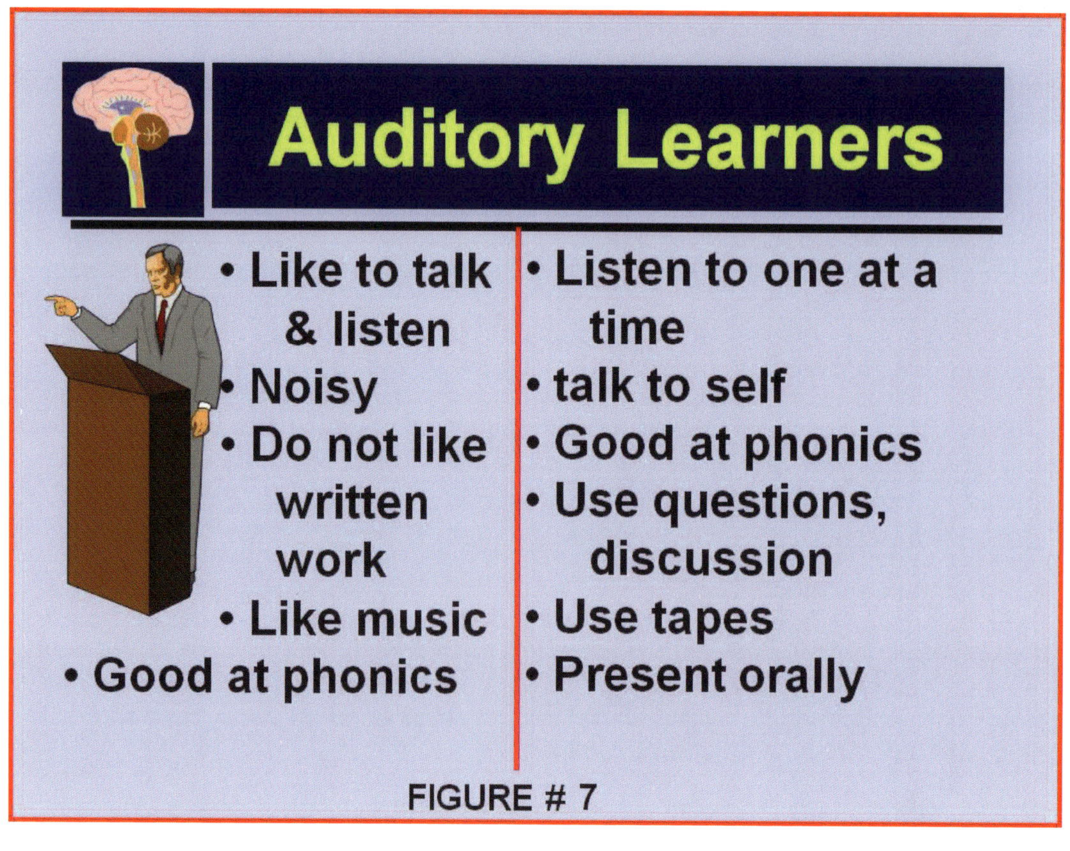

FIGURE # 7

providing learning options. Research is leading more and more of the best schools and colleges to move past a narrow focus on lectures and reading and to increase opportunities for both visual and project-based learning. Schools and colleges that increase learning options help many more students, especially those with right dominant preferences, to reach the levels of achievement and creativity desired by many employers.

Any teacher or school or college that does not provide learning style options cannot fully serve the needs of all talented learners. So, both students and parents can legitimately seek and promote attention to such options.

A more detailed way of looking at **learning styles** is to consider the basic ways that your brain can receive information. Four ways are shown in Figure #6 to the left - - auditory, visual, somatic, and reflective. Again, individuals vary in the degree to which they prefer these different ways of receiving information. Let us look at each way.

Figure #7 to the left summarizes information on people who like to receive information by hearing it, a left-brain characteristic. The common characteristics of **auditory learners** are shown on the left of Figure #7. Most important, effective ways for auditory learning are listed on the right of the figure. Here are some comments on the items listed:

1. **Listen to one at a time.** - - An auditory learner often finds it very distracting to try to listen to two sound sources at once. So, if you are an auditory learner, study in a quiet place. You do not want to be distracted by music, a radio, or people talking.

2. **Talk to yourself.** - - When reading, auditory learners often talk quietly to themselves. In reality, they are listening to themselves to process the information. There is nothing wrong with this unless it slows the process of reading at a time when speed is critical. If that happens, get some help from a reading specialist.

3. **Good at phonics.** - - Auditory learners often profit from phonics instruction in reading. Some students who are slow at reading, profit greatly from a special auditory training program that accelerates their auditory recognition and processing of sounds into images in the brain. In other words, auditory training can increase reading ability for those that are not natural auditory learners.

4. **Use questions and discussion.** - - If you learn well from hearing about things, ask questions and discuss topics with the teacher and other students.

5. **Use tapes.** - - Lectures and audio tapes or discs can be a good way to learn for auditory learners. Video can also help if clear dialogue and oral explanations are matched to the visuals.

6. **Present orally.** - - Auditory learners can often explain their learning best orally. When that is so, they should elect oral presentations when choices are offered. However, some learners like to receive information orally but prefer to present it to others in another way. So, analyze yourself carefully here. You will learn more about this when we get to multiple intelligences.

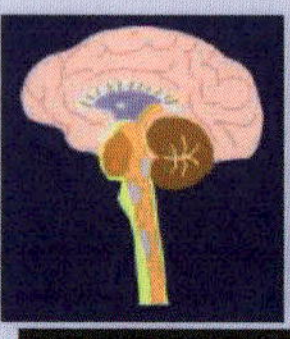

Visual Learners

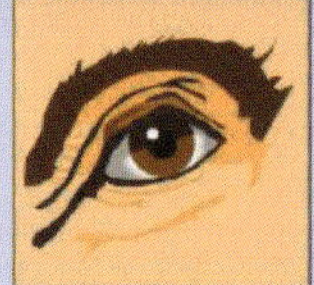

- Like visuals
- Like to know big picture
- Neat
- Like colors
- Not good at phonics
- Like multimedia, books, posters

- Use videos, charts
- Preview books
- Highlight, map, underline
- Use graphic organizers
- Draw pictures with written notes
- Construct visuals

FIGURE # 8

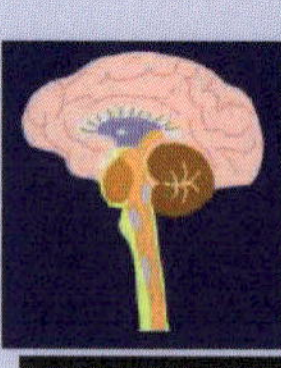

Styles in a Reading Lab

"Success Maker"

FIGURE # 9

If you prefer auditory learning, add some notes on that at the bottom of your TABLE #2 sheet. Continue this process of adding notes about yourself to your TABLE #2 sheet as you review the remaining learning styles. Get to know and use your style preferences.

Study Figure #8 on **visual learners**. Again, characteristics of visual learners are listed on the left and common ways of learning are listed on the right of the figure. Here are comments on the listed ways of visual learning:

1. **Use videos charts.** - - An explanatory video or picture is often necessary for visual learners. .Also, clear explanatory videos, computer programs, pictures, and charts are extremely valuable to a majority of learners including those who are not clearly visual learners. Do not neglect the value of such learning aids no matter what learning style you prefer. Figure #9 to the left shows two learners in the reading lab described earlier.

2. **Preview books.** - - To get the big picture; look at the table of contents and chapter headings in a book before you read for details. In a book like this one, you can get the big picture by looking at the left graphic pages and first paragraphs of each chapter before reading for detail. In class, ask your teacher if he or she can give you a brief overview of each new unit before starting on details.

3. **Highlight, map, underline.** - - Highlighting or underlining important points in your notes or even in a book that you own (not in one that must be returned to the school) are important visual cues for reviewing and remembering. Mapping is any process of **drawing relationships between important items of information; see the next item.**

4. **Use graphic organizers.** - - You can buy great books on mind mapping, a way of drawing a picture map of a concept or story or event. Such maps help you to remember important information. One of the best books for help in this area is VISUAL THINKING: TOOLS FOR MAPPING YOUR IDEAS by Nancy Margulies and Christine Valenza. It is available on Amazon.com. For now, below this list, we shall cover some very easy to use graphic organizers.

5. **Draw pictures with written notes.** - - Teachers usually help you to learn to prepare outline summaries as notes from lectures or reading. If you are a visual learner, it helps to add small hand drawn pictures or images to those notes. One way of doing this is to draw a line down the center of your notes page. Place your written notes or outline on one side of the center line and draw related reminder images on the other side of the center line. Do not worry about being an artist; your small drawings (even of words) are whatever works as reminders for you.

6. **Construct visuals.** - - Visual learners can often explain their learning best with pictures or drawings. For example, my daughter explained the history of the westward movement in the United States by pasting a collage of pictures on a large poster board that her teacher could then use for future classes.

Remember, visual learning can be very useful even for many auditory and somatic learners.

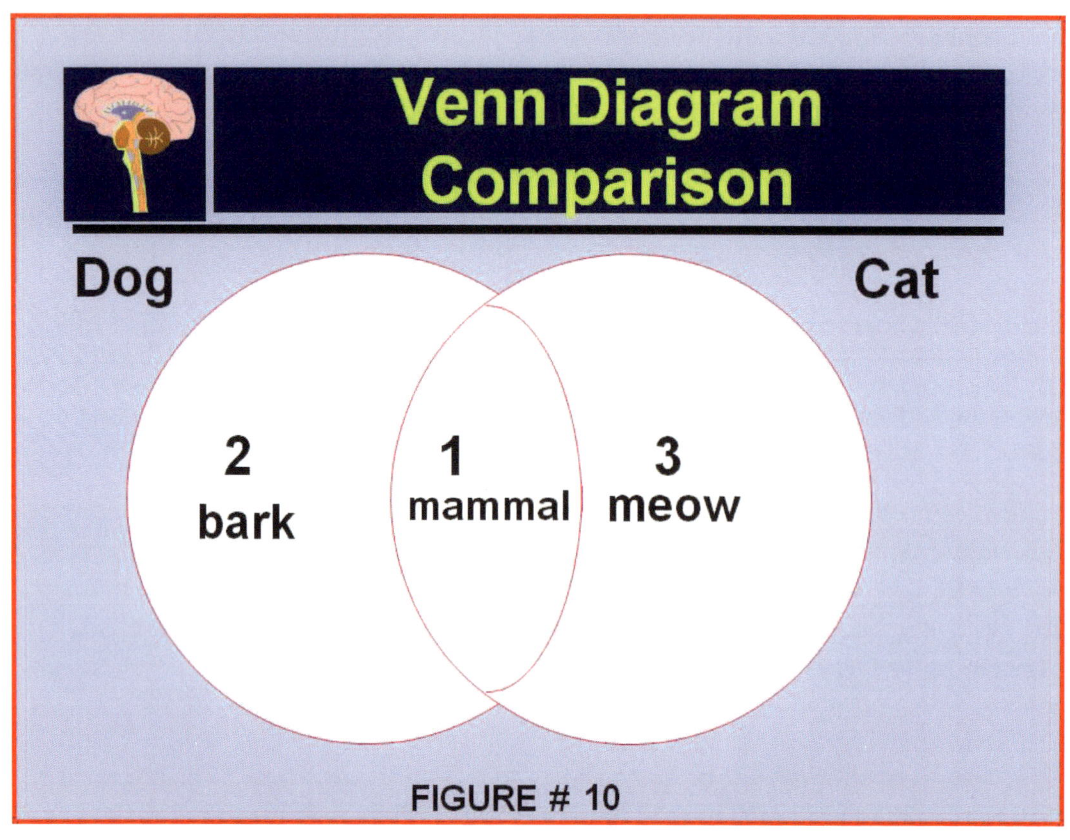

FIGURE # 10

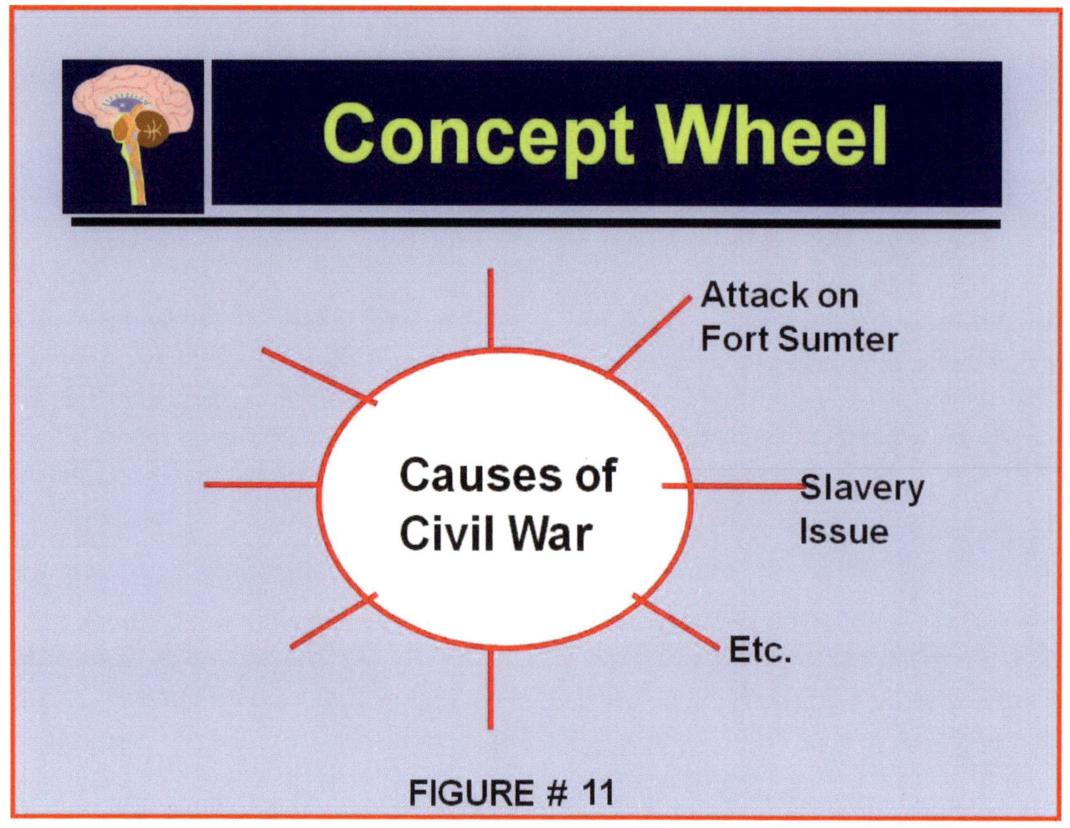

FIGURE # 11

Now let us review some easy to use graphic organizers. Figure #10 shows a Venn diagram that you might have been taught to use to help you remember comparisons in elementary school. It consists of two overlapping circles. When comparing, you place similarities of two items in the overlap and differences in the opposite non-overlapping parts of the circles. There are two other simple but powerful visual organizers that can help you to remember patterns of relationships.

In the concept wheel shown in Figure #11 to the left, you place a topic title in the center. The example here is CAUSES OF THE CIVIL WAR. As you read or listen and discover causes, you list each on a different spoke of the wheel; two examples are shown. If you are a visual learner, this drawing will really help you to remember the information.

Figure #12 below is an even more powerful organizer for remembering causes of certain efforts or results. It is also called a fishbone chart because it is shaped like the skeleton of a fish. The causes of the Civil War example can be used here too. CIVIL WAR could be placed where the word RESULT is now. Each of the causes could be placed in a fishbone box. In the next chapter, we shall review another use of this diagram. For now, just be aware that graphic or visual organizers can be very helpful for learning and remembering, especially for but not limited to visual learners.

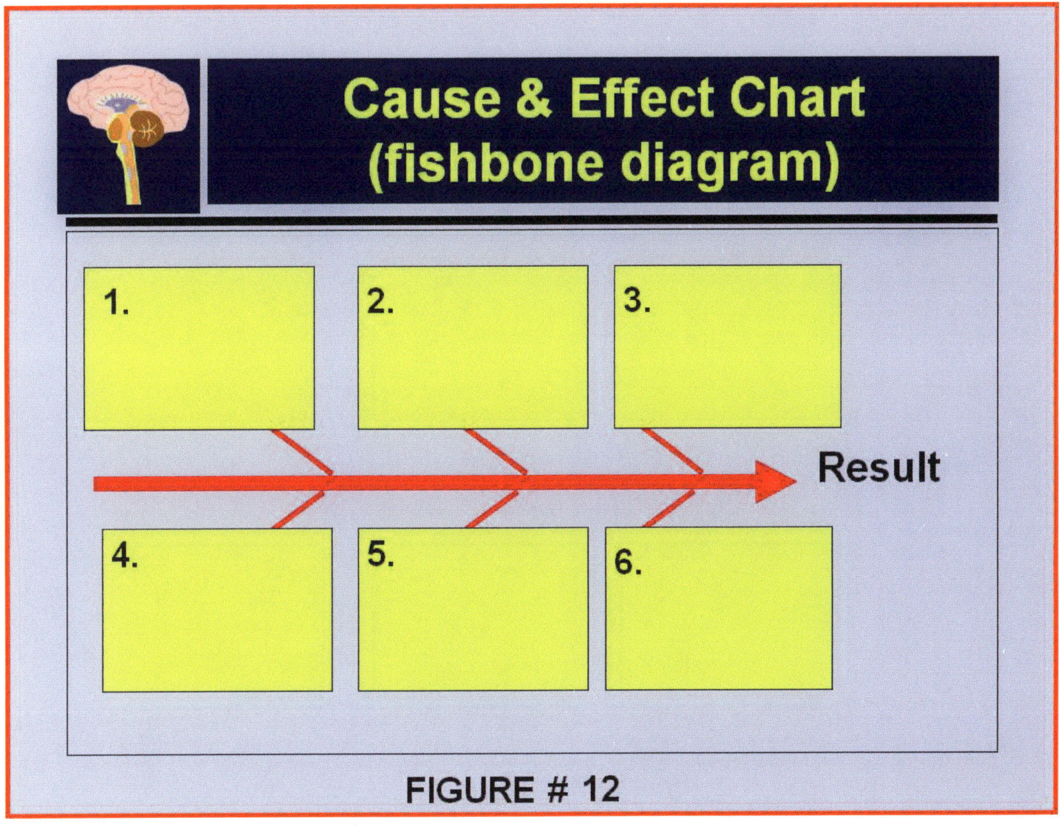

FIGURE # 12

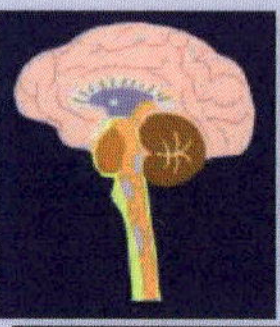

Somatic Learners

- Like doing & moving
- Often athletic
- Find it difficult to sit still
- Use gestures and touching
- Like short answer tests

- Use projects
- Work with materials
- Use drama & moving
- Use multimedia
- Make & show models & give demonstrations

FIGURE # 13

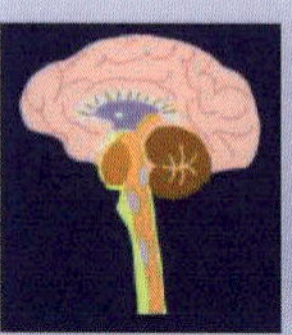

Be Aware...

The brain tends to remember meaningful information.

FIGURE # 14

Practice using the graphic organizers in this section of the booklet when you are taking notes while reading homework or studying for tests. You will find that the visual framework will help you to learn and remember six or seven major points about any issue, story, or process. According to research, it is best not to exceed seven supporting points in one graphic or diagram.

Now, review Figure #13 on **somatic learners**. The word "somatic" refers to the body. There are really two types of somatic learning. Kinesthetic refers to body movement such as learning to ride a bike. Tactile refers to touch such as learning about something by handling it or building it. Characteristics of somatic learners are shown on the left of Figure #13. Here are comments on the somatic ways of learning listed on the right side of the figure:

1. **Use projects.** - - Somatic learners often learn best from doing projects. They like the moving and hands-on way of learning.

2. **Work with materials.** - - Using equipment and doing experiments helps somatic learners.

3. **Use drama and moving.** - - The action and motion of being in a play or simulation game will help you learn. Sitting still too long can be very difficult for kinesthetic learners.

4. **Use multimedia.** - - Interactive computer programs with which you must move and elect actions are useful for somatic learning. This is why somatic learners like hand-held electronic games.

5. **Make and show models and give demonstrations.** - - Making and showing and demonstrating involve touching (tactile) and moving (kinesthetic) action. So, if you are a somatic learner, look for opportunities to demonstrate your learning that way.

No figure is provided for **reflective learning** because it is really the result of internal thinking about information received from auditory, visual, and/or somatic actions. Our next chapter will cover thinking and using information. Here I simply want you to consider that you can <u>receive</u> new information from the thinking process. For example, if you take the somatic and visual action of doing a survey as a class project then analyze or think about what the results of your survey mean, your conclusions are new information that you received from thinking and not by hearing or seeing or touching. So reflection or thinking is an important way of constructing and therefore receiving new information!

Before closing this chapter here are some more researched facts for you to consider for your learning:

1. Figure #14 to the left asks you to be aware that **you tend to remember information that has practical value or meaning for you.** Think about recent homework you have been given in school. From which assignments did you remember the most; from which, the least?

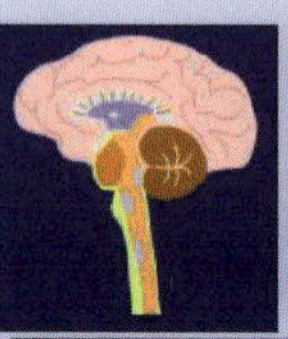

Real-life Tasks

~~Write 3 paragraphs that are properly constructed according to our standards (with topic sentences, supporting sentences, and accurate grammar and spelling).~~

Write paragraphs that are properly constructed according to our standards and that another class member can use to program our VCR so that it automatically records the news at 6 p.m. tonight.

FIGURE # 15

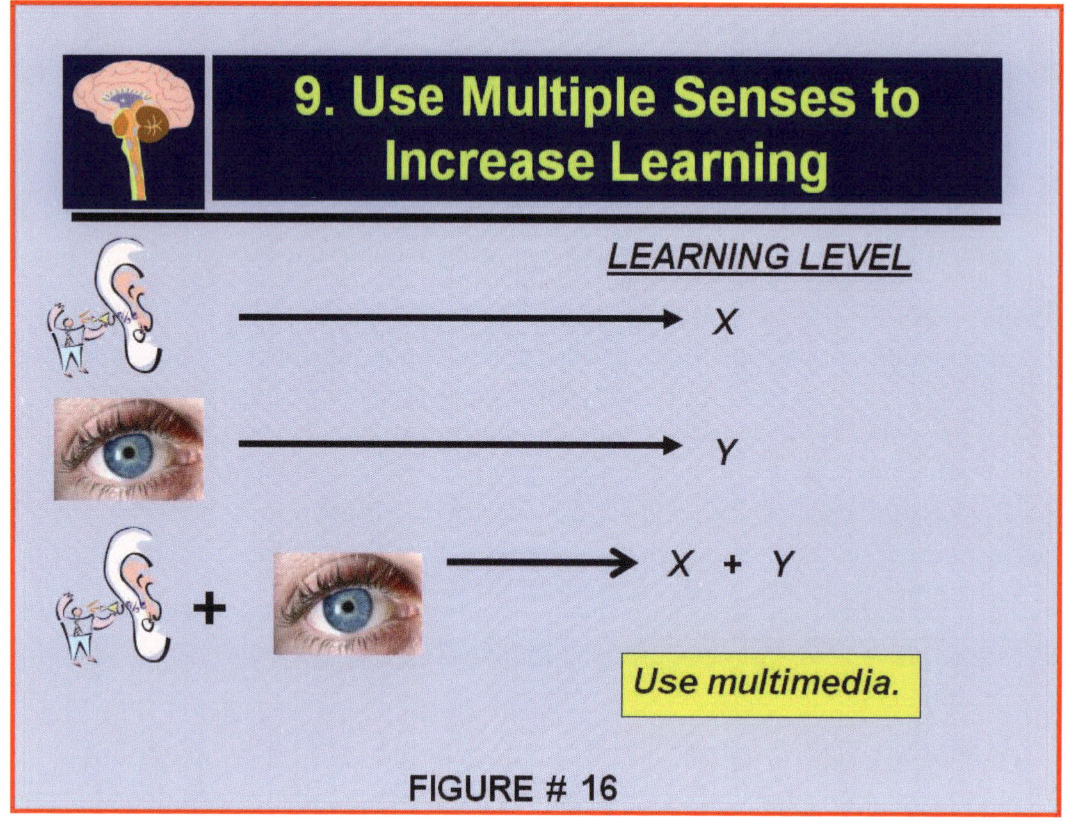

FIGURE # 16

Figure #15 provides a writing assignment example. If a teacher gave you the assignment described on the left of Figure #15, it could be boring and quickly forgotten. If the teacher gave you the real life assignment on the right of Figure #15, you would tend to remember the learning because it would have a practical or real life or more meaningful outcome. Your writing would or would not be clear enough for another member of the class to use the VCR properly! Ask your teacher to help you understand the practical value of what you are asked to learn.

2. Figure #16 to the left makes another important point. **Using multiple senses to learn something will usually result in more effective learning than using one sense.** If you learn to level X with hearing and to level Y with seeing, then coordinated hearing and seeing could help you to reach a much higher level of learning such as X + Y. This is why multimedia computer software that requires you to see and to hear and even to move to make choices can be so effective for learning.

3. Figure #17 below makes some additional important points:

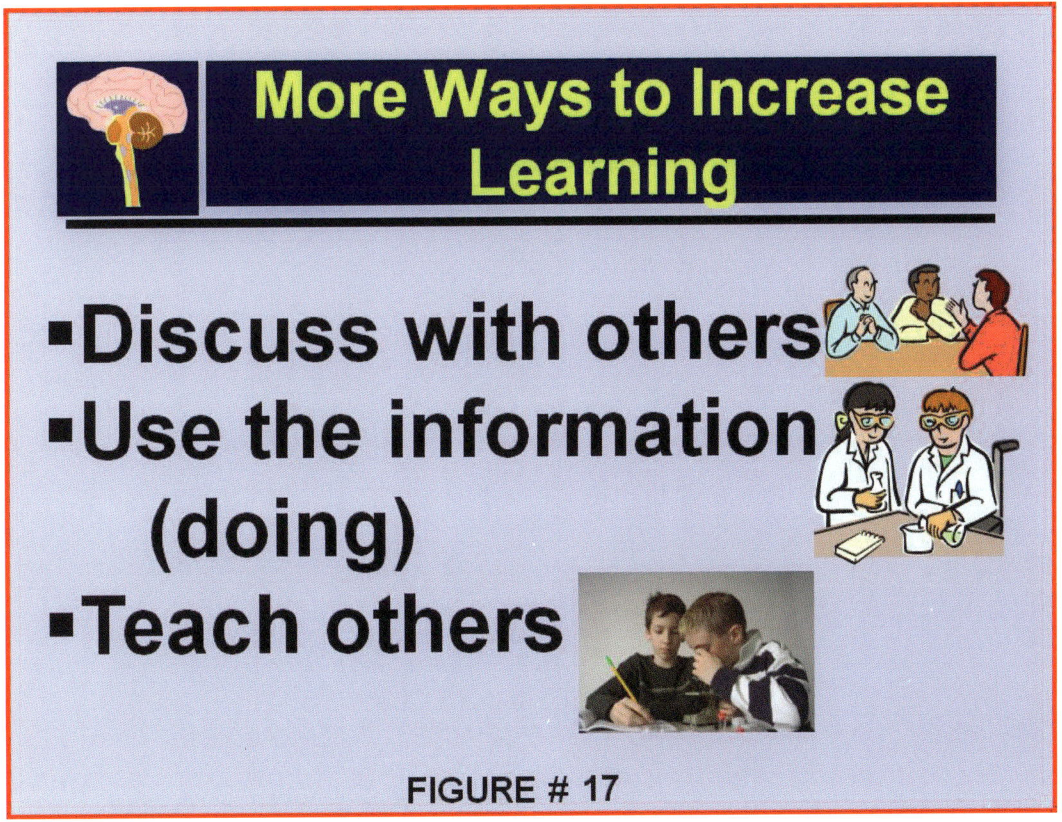

FIGURE # 17

a. Discussion with others can help you to learn from each other, especially for right brain learners.

b. Using information to do something helps learning because it gives meaning to the information.

TABLE #3: MY PERSONAL LEARNING CHOICES

Summary of My Preferences	
My results on a left-right brain test. Circle one item.	Left dominant Right dominant Nearly balanced
My top three preferred characteristics from Table #2.	1. 2. 3.
My favorite learning advice items from Table #2.	1. 2. 3.
My dominant learning style. Circle one (or two if tied) item.	Auditory Visual Somatic
Major learning suggestions I liked from the auditory, visual, somatic lists.	1. 2. 3.
What graphic organizer seem most useful to you? Circle one.	Venn diagram Concept wheel Cause & Effect chart
Circle any item that seems to really help you learn.	Assignments that relate to real life To both see and hear new material Discussion with others Teaching others

c. Teaching others is a way to learn the most yourself because you are discussing and using the information.

Watch for opportunities to use the power of these added facts such as studying with a friend before a test.

Finally, keep these two points in mind on learning styles. First, whenever you are having a difficult time studying or learning, try to switch to your most preferred learning style. This might mean asking the teacher for special help in that regard or, for example if you are a visual learner, buying a book that gives you visual help in a subject. Second, remember to practice developing skills in the learning styles you do not prefer. At times, it will be necessary to use those other styles for certain school or work tasks.

Review Questions for Chapter 2

Mark an L for left-brain or an R for right-brain or an S for somatic after each of these characteristics:

1. Prefers images and pictures.
2. Focuses on details.
3. Enjoys learning by doing projects.
4. Enjoys auditory learning.
5. Is spontaneous and random.

Answers can be found in the Appendix.

A Special Summary Exercise

You have completed reviewing half of this booklet. This is a good time to summarize what you have learned about yourself. Have someone make you a photocopy of TABLE #3 to the left. Then complete each item in the right-hand column according to the directions or question in the left-hand column. When you add the test results that you will gain in Chapter #4, you will have a very useful picture of the way YOU learn best. Use the information to capitalize on your learning style strengths and to guide practice in any areas where you should improve. Knowing and improving your learning skills can be a great investment in your future success.

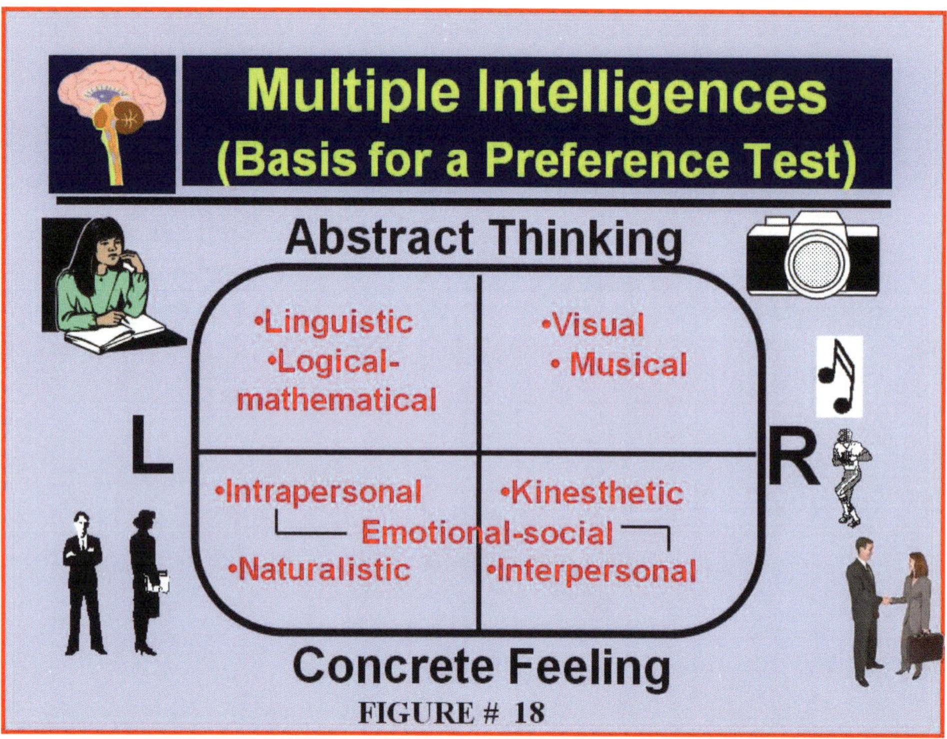

FIGURE # 18

Figure #18 lists some multiple intelligences or talents in four quadrants corresponding to our simplified brain model. The two quadrants on the left represent the left brain. The two on the right represent the right brain. The top two quadrants represent the upper brain or cerebrum where abstract thinking occurs. The bottom two quadrants represent the lower brain and its concentration on hands-on or concrete thinking and feelings. We shall continue using this model for convenience even though we know that the different parts of the brain work together and that one part can even take over for another part that is damaged. Watch for the same four part model as you proceed in the booklet.

CHAPTER 3

Processing and Using Information

Once your brain has received and stored information, you can think about it and use it. This is when your intelligences or talents become important. Note the plural of the word "intelligence" here. Dr. Howard Gardner at Harvard University has identified at least nine intelligences in his now famous theory of **multiple intelligences**. Eight of the nine are shown with dots in Figure #18 shown at the left. The figure also lists another intelligence or talent called emotional intelligence which we shall discuss later; it is related to a combination of interpersonal and intrapersonal intelligence.

Here is a brief description of the intelligences identified by Dr. Gardner:

1. **Linguistic** - - Concerned with words, sounds, reading, and language. Journalists and lawyers use this intelligence.

2. **Logical-Mathematical** - - Concerned with numbers and logic. Accountants and computer programmers use this talent. NOTE: The first two talents described are the only two measured by many old-fashioned intelligence tests.

3. **Visual** - - Concerned with pictures, patterns and images. Artists, designers, and photographers function with this talent. Also visualization talent is helpful in nearly every field. For example, a great baseball hitter often "sees" or imagines what he is going to do before he does it. Some successful entrepreneurs can imagine the outcome of a particular plan before they pursue it. Some of our greatest scientists, like Albert Einstein, visualized their theories before working on the mathematical details.

4. **Musical** - - Concerned with rhythms and melodies. (The right type of music can also be very helpful in certain language learning with some students.)

5. **Kinesthetic** - - Concerned with body movements and handling objects. Mechanics, surgeons, craftspeople, athletes, and dancers function with this talent.

6. **Interpersonal** - - Concerned with understanding and working effectively with other people. Social workers, teachers, and negotiators need this talent to be most effective.

7. **Intrapersonal** - - Concerned with self-understanding. Leaders and self-employed business people who prefer to work alone on their goals often depend on this talent.

8. **Naturalistic** - - Concerned with observing, classifying, and understanding the parts of the physical environment.

9. **Philosophical-ethical** - - Concerned with sensitivity to different cultural environments and to moral and ethical issues. This one is NOT listed in Figure #18.

Each of us has all nine intelligences, or more. However, most people have one or two dominant intelligences or talents. Also, it is possible to develop or improve an intelligence or talent area.

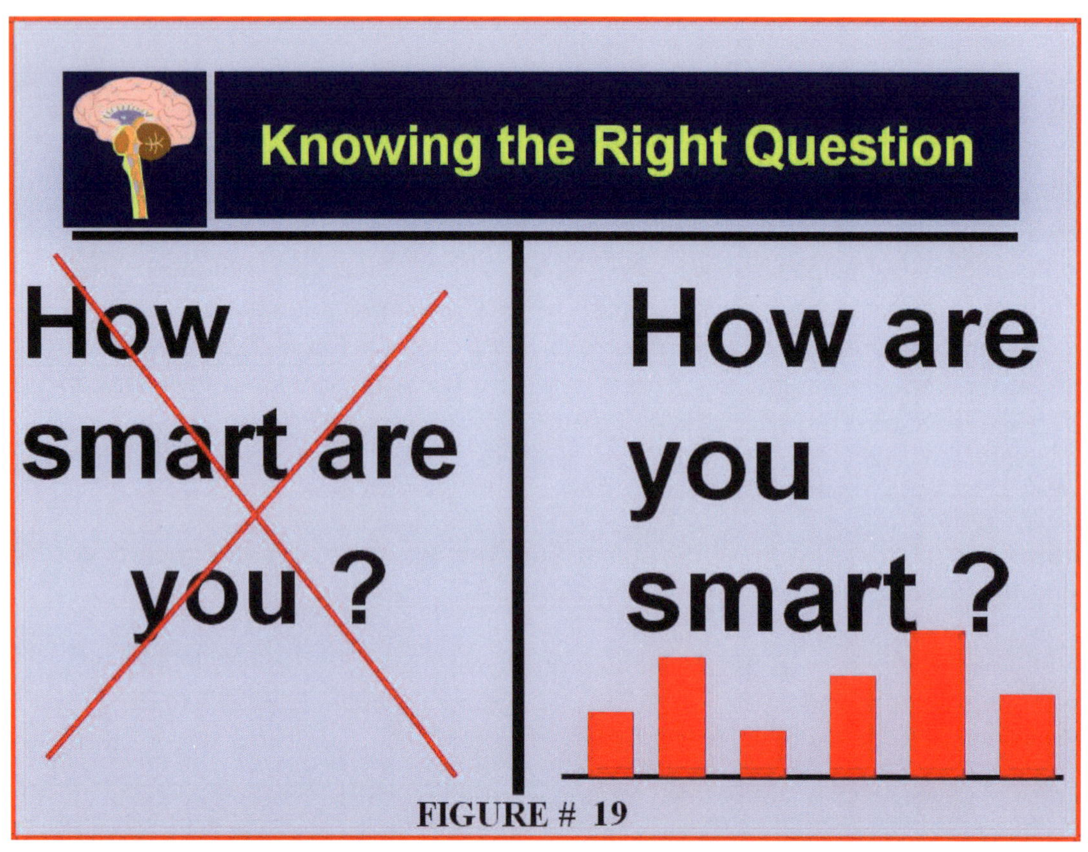

FIGURE # 19

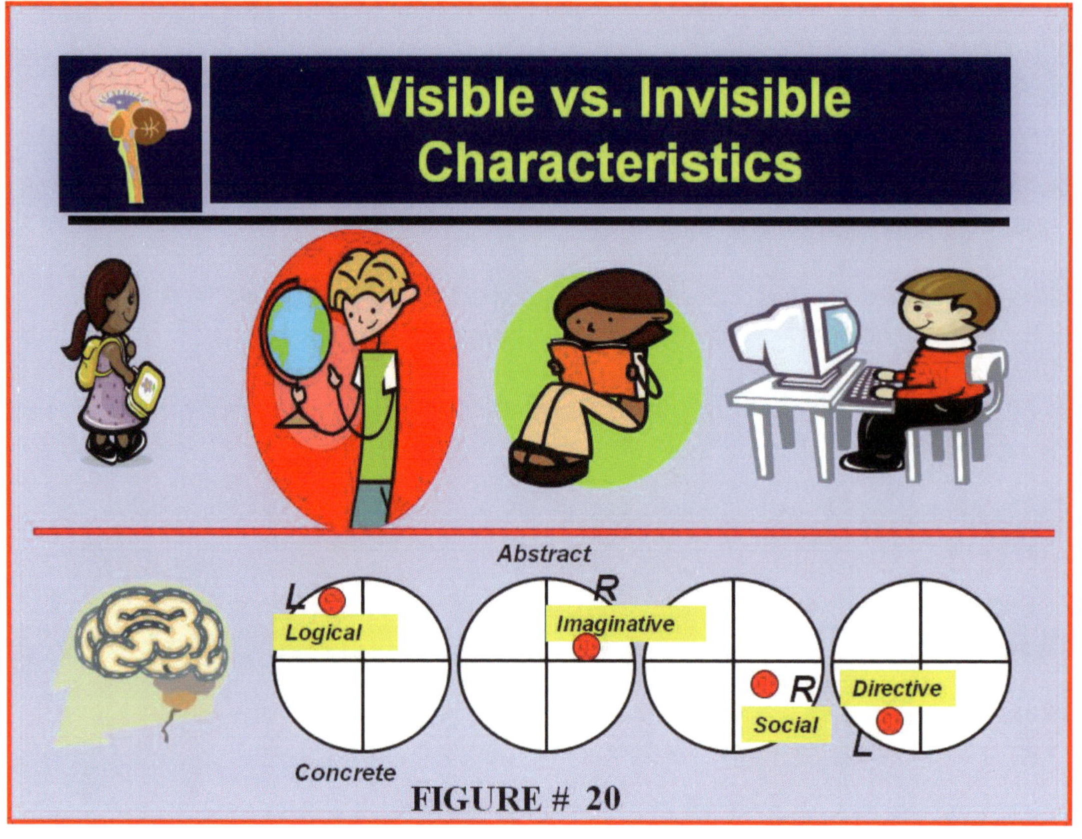

FIGURE # 20

Here are important points to remember about intelligences:

1. They are used for processing or thinking about information and for using information to produce conclusions, performances, or products. They are NOT receiving or learning styles. For example, a visual learning style is a preference for receiving information visually. However visual intelligence is a talent for thinking about things visually as Einstein did or for producing visual representations like a painting. A person who has a visual learning style might or might not have a strong visual talent for thinking about or using information.

2. You can gain an advantage by selecting school majors and career positions that use your strongest intelligences or talents since there is no such reality as having only one intelligence. The one intelligence myth came from old intelligence tests that measured primarily only two of the intelligences as previously stated. Look at Figure #19. We no longer say "How smart are you?" We now know that each person has his or her individual strengths in different talents as symbolized by the bar graph on the right of Figure #19 where each bar stands for a different intelligence. If a person does not seem to be talented in math, he or she might be a whiz in one or two other intelligences. So today, the correct question is "How are you smart?" Anyone who belittles someone with a weakness in some talents is really showing their own ignorance. Figure #20 helps you to remember this point - - Just as individuals differ in exterior or visual characteristics (height, weight, etc.), they differ in the strengths of different invisible intelligences like logical, imaginative (visual), social (interpersonal), and directive (intrapersonal). Respect the invisible talents of others.

3. However, you can and should grow or improve the intelligences that you do not naturally prefer because different intelligences work together to solve many problems. For example, after being trained in visual thinking, one class of third grade students doubled its average test score on a second version of a test as the students were able to visualize and think about word problems more effectively. The visual intelligence of the students worked with their logic-mathematical intelligence.

4. Paying attention to your preferred intelligences can have a major impact on your future. People who drift into a career path that is not compatible with their preferred intelligences are often very unhappy in their work. Those whose careers make use of their talents and preferences often truly enjoy their work. Every high school, college, and employer should help you to match to a career path that you will enjoy. However, if they do not help, be sure to consider this matching very carefully yourself. Chapter 4 will give you specific help on this.

TABLE #4 on the next page shows activities grouped under each of eight intelligences. You can use the listing to identify one or more intelligences that you believe are your strengths OR to identify activities that you could practice to strengthen one or more of your intelligences. Study this table very carefully to decide which intelligence and related activity areas appeal to you the most. In the next chapter, you will find a brain test that will give you more help on analyzing your brain preferences and on using that information. As you analyze the table on

TABLE #4: EIGHT INTELLIGENCES AND RELATED ACTIVITIES

LOGICAL-MATHEMATICAL	VISUAL
Interpreting patterns Debating, Preparing jokes Playing word games Calculating or computer programming	Using mind mapping Using a computer graphic program Preparing visual stories or aids Preparing video or computer Presentations Drawing or making models
AUDITORY-LINGUISTIC	**MUSICAL**
Giving a speech Writing a story or report Solving puzzles Reading or writing	Singing Composing Playing an instrument Keeping time to a beat Using music for learning
INTRAPERSONAL	**INTERPERSONAL**
Listing goals Leading a team Meditating Writing poetry Analyzing your styles and/or talents	Working in teams Teaching or helping others Hosting an event Persuading or "selling" to others
NATURALISTIC	**KINESTHETIC**
Observing and recording Collecting Classifying or identifying Experimenting Forecasting	Participating in movement exercises Dancing Building and fixing Acting Taking field trips for analysis

page 26, remember the meaning of the word "preference." You might not yet be very talented in a particular intelligence area, but you might prefer (like) to become talented in that area. Since an intelligence or talent can be developed or improved, consider any area which you like in TABLE #4 even though you might not yet be really talented in that area. Ask yourself two questions. First, ask" What are my strongest areas?" Second, ask **"In which area in TABLE #4 to the left would I like to grow my talent?"**

Next, let us look at **emotional intelligence** which is a combination of intrapersonal intelligence (self-understanding) and interpersonal intelligence (understanding and working effectively with others.) The following five questions and answers will help you to understand and grow your emotional intelligence:

Question #1. - - Why is emotional intelligence important? The powerful answer is that a person's emotional intelligence or EI is often the most important factor in determining success or failure in a career path. Putting aside downsizing in a weakening economy, more employees are fired or fail to gain promotions because they have failed to develop their EI than for any other reason.

Question #2. - - What is emotional Intelligence? It is a person's ability to deal with his or her own emotions and the emotions of others in a constructive manner, a manner that promotes teamwork and productivity rather than conflict. Perhaps, most importantly, it is an ability that can be learned and "grown" just like other intelligences. Before going to Question #3, consider this imaginary situation. You are a clerk in a retail store. A very angry customer comes to you and very loudly yells that "I am here to return this piece of junk you sold to me!" The customer is carrying a toaster he bought the day before. You must now decide how to respond. Which of these two responses would you select? Before you answer, discuss that question with a family member or other friend and consider the facts below the responses.

RESPONSE A	RESPONSE B
Sir, we do not sell junk, and I do not like your yelling at me. Calm down.	Sir, I am sorry something is wrong. Tell me about it, and I am sure we can correct the situation for you.

Here are some relevant facts. First, your job as an employee in the store is to service customers in a way that gets them to return and to buy again. Second, the customer might have a very legitimate reason for his anger. Third, if someone is very angry and you start by just suggesting that they get over it, you can expect the anger to increase. Fourth, continued confrontation with an angry customer is not apt to positively impress your supervisor. Your skill in dealing with situations like this will undoubtedly affect your future employment! Remember, you are the store's representative. Fifth, your response will determine what happens next. Now, what do you want to happen next? After you make your decision think about one last question - **- Do you see why emotional intelligence as a person expresses it in their communications often determines their success or failure in a career area that involves interaction with others?** Now, continue to Question #3.

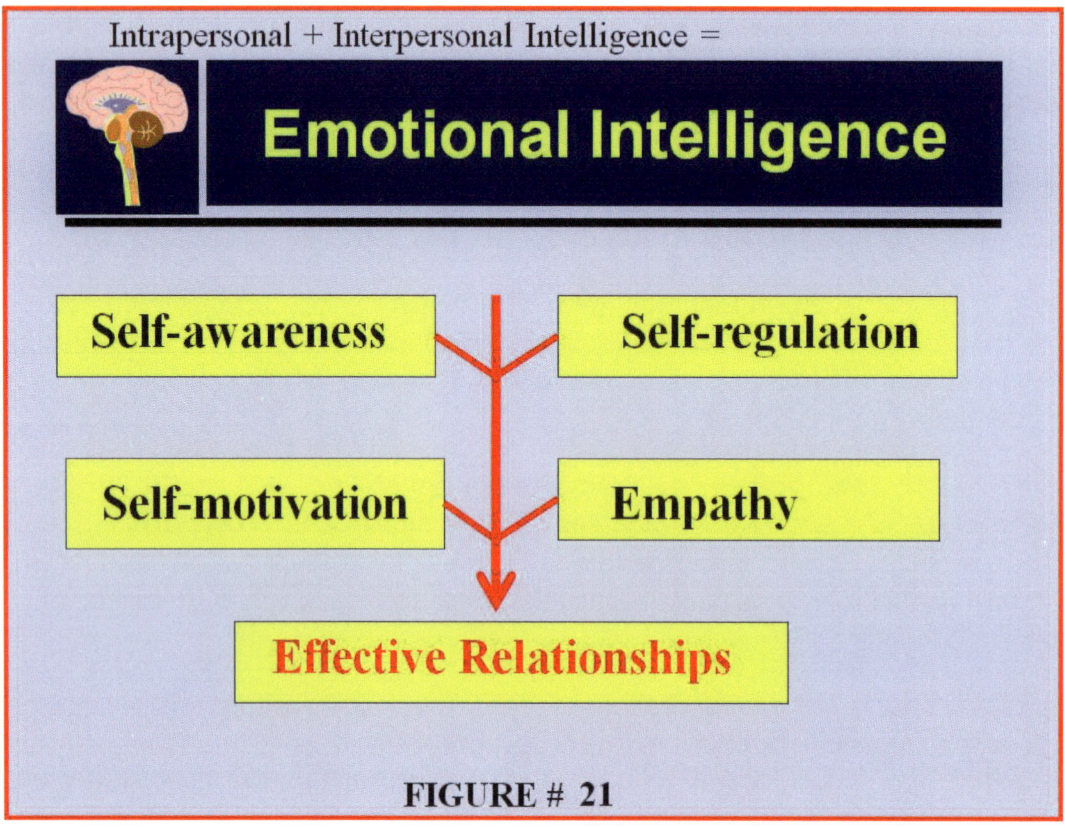

FIGURE # 21

The description of using emotional intelligence on page 28 relates to career success. However, remember that the same skills apply to communication with family members, friends, and even strangers. When someone says something to you, stop and think about EI skills. Decide whether the response you are about to make is apt to promote positive or negative feelings in the person to whom you are going to respond. Then decide what you want to happen. Developing skills in this area can make you a pleasant person as opposed to being perceived as thoughtless and unpleasant.

Question #3. - - How can you recognize emotional intelligence? The most direct way to answer this is to describe what you will see if a person is exhibiting a high level of the five basic components of EI. The person will show these skills that are listed in Figure #21:

a. **Self-awareness** - - The person recognizes his or her emotions and the causes of same.
b. **Self-regulation** - - The person, armed with self-awareness, controls his or her actions carefully rather than just reacting to a situation solely on the basis of impulse generated by an emotion-producing event. This is not a matter of denying or hiding emotions but rather of not being ruled by emotions.
c. **Self-motivation** - - When something goes wrong, the high EI person does not ask "What is wrong with me or us?" He or she asks "What can I (or we) fix?"
d. **Empathy** - - The person exhibits interest and an ability in recognizing the feelings of others. Empathy is the ability to "walk in the other person's shoes."
e. **Effective relationships** - - Using the previously listed four skills, the person communicates with others in a way that addresses their as well as his or her needs. The emphasis is on solving problems together, not on unnecessary confrontation. The high EI person communicates with a constructive goal in mind.

Question #4. - - How can a person develop strong emotional intelligence?

a. See if your school has a learning program in this area. If so, enroll.

b. Read, study, and discuss materials on EI. Use Google and Amazon.com to find the materials. Discuss them with your parents and peers.

c. Volunteer for and practice the interpersonal and intrapersonal activities listed previously in TABLE #3. Have the goal of generating positive responses from others when you communicate.

d. Observe and analyze person-to-person interactions every day at school and at home, especially when you are involved. Ask yourself questions like these:

(1) Did I or the other person(s) understand (self-awareness) and control (self-regulation) personal emotions?

(2) Did I or the other person(s) have the goal (self-motivation) of solving problems?

(3) Was I or the other person sensitive to the feelings and emotions of others (empathy)?

(4) Before reacting to others, did I pause and think about what comments might contribute to solving rather than causing problems?

(5) Am I consciously attempting to improve my EI and my relationships with others?

None of this is meant to imply that you should be either devious or condescending in your communications to others. Honesty and your right to expect fairness from others are part of good communication skills that can build positive relationships with others. However, always

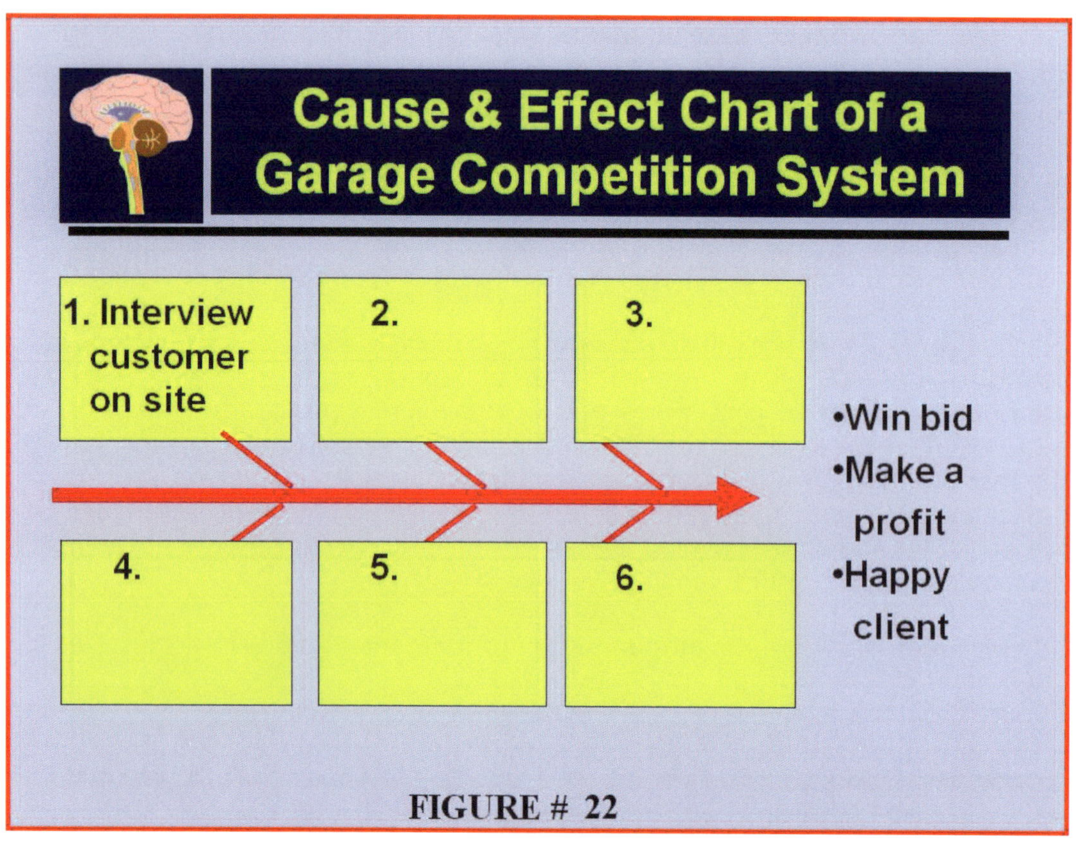

FIGURE # 22

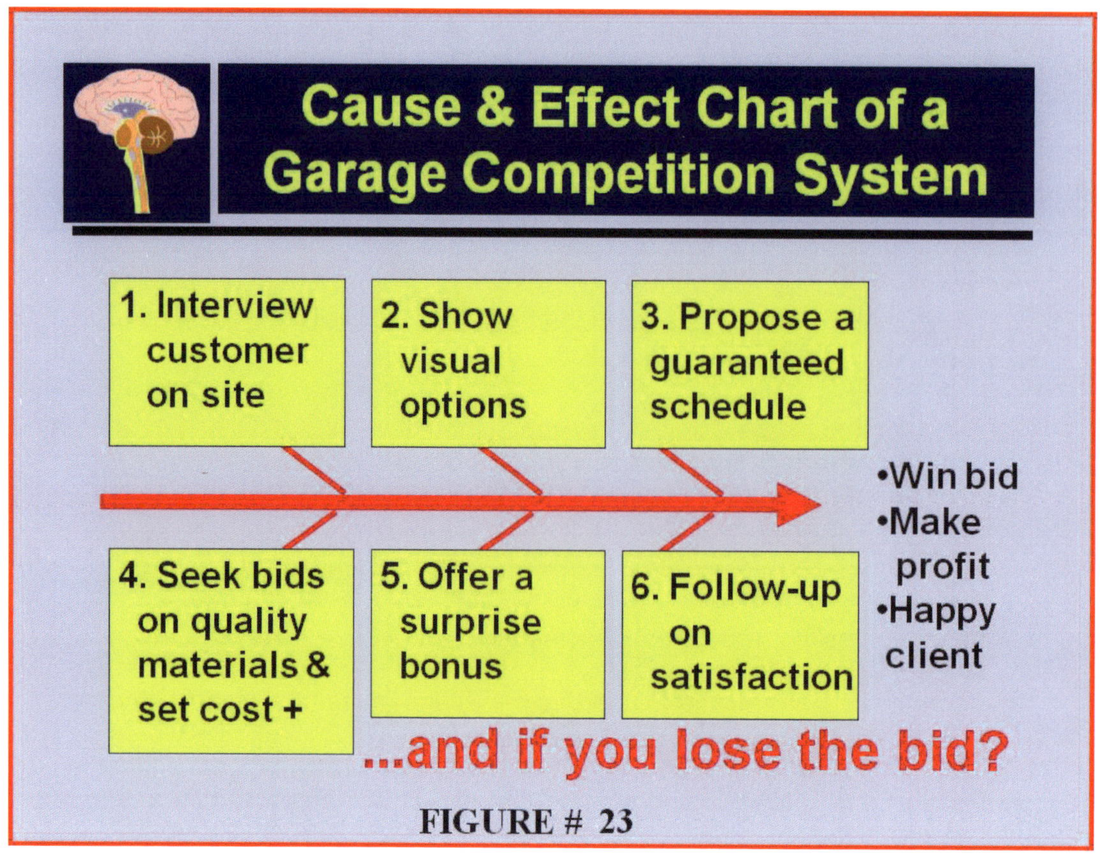

FIGURE # 23

remember that every communication to others can be either sensitive and constructive or insensitive and unnecessarily confrontational. That is your choice, and it will affect your future.

Finally, I end this chapter with another suggestion for use of the **cause and effect chart** introduced in Chapter 2. Look at Figure #22. It shows a study assignment I gave a team of high school students who were asked to pretend that they were partners in a company that builds garages. A lady had telephoned the company and asked for a bid on building a garage for her vehicle. The team's assignment was to fill-in the boxes with descriptions of actions that would lead to the results shown to the right of the arrow. I had filled-in one box as an example. This is not a map for listing facts you are learning as it was in the previous chapter in learning styles. Here **the diagram is a tool used to visualize or plan actions that might lead to desired results.** This use of the visual planning tool is so important because using it regularly helps the pre-frontal lobes develop their ability to predict or plan at just the right time (teenage) in the development of the brain. When you develop this ability in the pre-frontal lobes, you tend to think in advance about the potential consequences of certain actions. This can help you to plan for success and to avoid thoughtless actions (like reckless driving) that can lead to disaster. Use this tool as often as you can. Figure #23 shows one set of ideas generated by this assignment. Then I added a new question - - Tell me what you would do if you lose the bid? (Ask the lady why you lost so that you can improve your next bid.) Can you see how a cause and effect diagram or map can help you to use visual thinking and to develop valuable prediction or planning skills?

Review Questions for Chapter 3

1. Which does intelligence do?

    a. Receive information

    or

    b. Process or use information

2. What intelligence is concerned with understanding yourself?
3. How many of the nine or more intelligences did old-fashioned intelligence tests measure?
4. What intelligence is a major factor in most career success?
5. What tool can be very useful for aiding visual thinking?

Answers can be found in the Appendix.

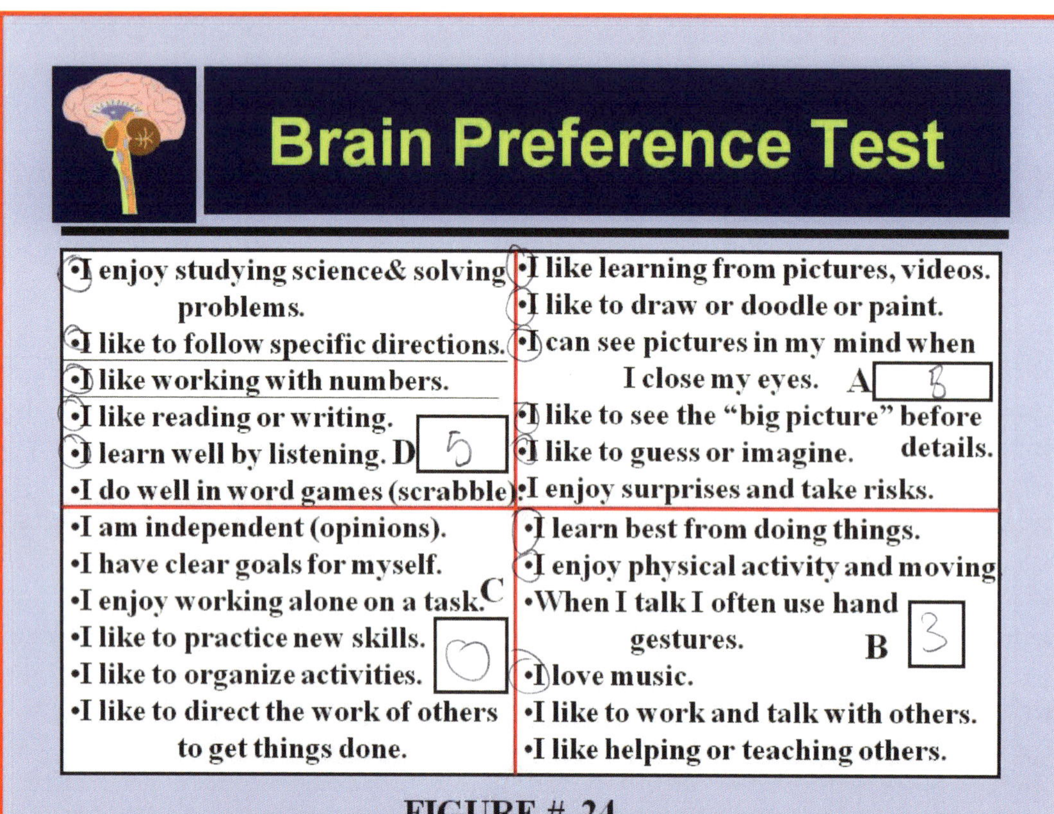

FIGURE # 24

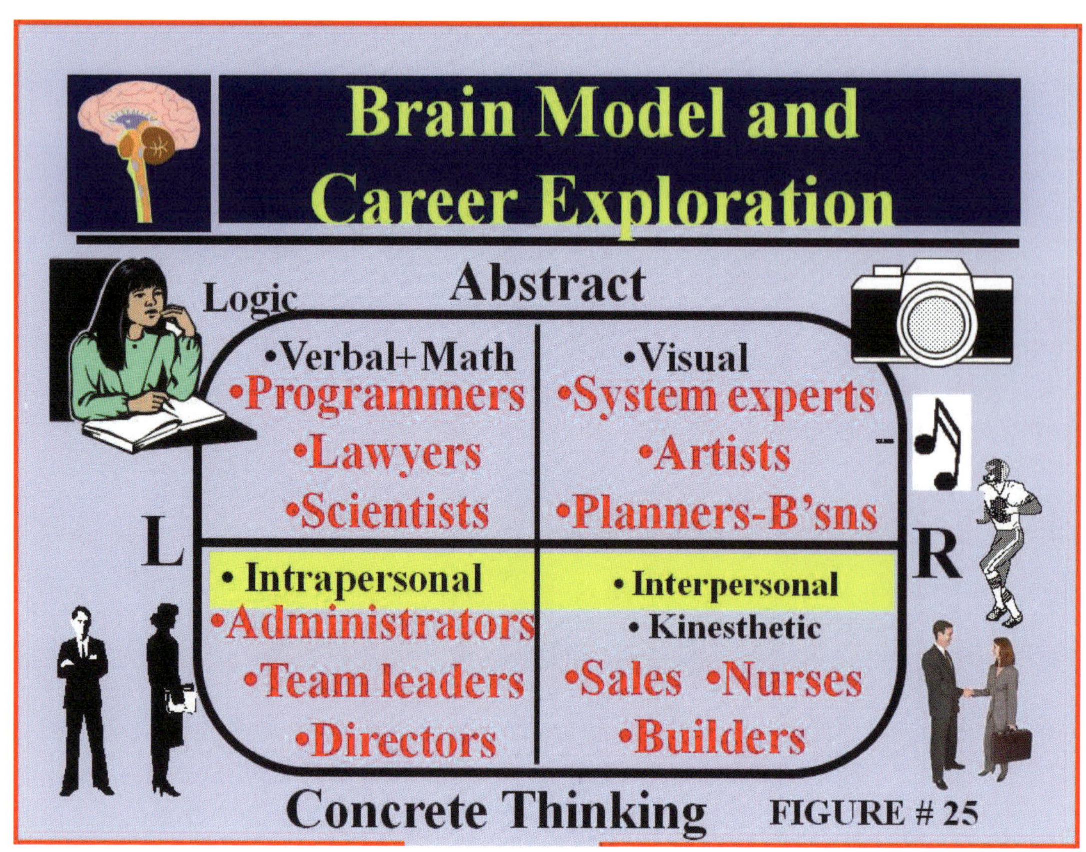

FIGURE # 25

Chapter 4

Learning More about YOUR Brain

Do you remember Figure #18 that listed some multiple intelligences in four quadrants or parts of our simplified brain model? If not, turn back to page 21 and review that picture. Now look at Figure #24 to the left. It is a four part **Brain Preference Test** based on questions related to the earlier Figure #18. Take the test following the directions below:

<u>Directions for the Preference Test</u>

1. Read each statement in a quadrant (one of the four large sections in Figure #24).
2. Check or circle the dot before any statement that really describes YOU. For example in the upper left quadrant D, if you usually or always enjoy science, check the first statement in that quadrant. If you do not enjoy science or often do not enjoy it, do NOT check the first statement. When you finish with each statement in quadrant D, count the number of statements you have checked and place that number or score in the small box labeled D.
3. Repeat this process for each quadrant, marking your scores in the appropriate small boxes. There is no right or wrong answer for any statement, just your quick and honest estimate of whether or not the statement is usually accurate for you.
4. The quadrant in which you gain the highest score or number of statements selected is your dominant quadrant. Some folks get tie or close scores in two or more quadrants.

The two left quadrants, D and C, represent left brain intelligences and learning styles. The two right quadrants, A and B, represent right brain intelligences and learning styles. The two top quadrants, D and A, cover abstract thinking using words, numbers, pictures. The two bottom quadrants, C and B, cover concrete thinking and feelings focused more on practical doing. You can tell this from the questions. Also, be aware that the questions mix what you previously learned about styles and intelligences. For example, in quadrant A you might have selected the first statement which is a visual learning style but not have selected the second statement which is about visual intelligence or talent. So be sure that you analyze your response to individual questions and not just to quadrant scores.

For the most part the results of this test should verify statements that you recorded in Table #3 on learning styles and that you discovered on YOUR multiple intelligences in Chapter 3. With this complete picture, you can now make important decisions about your learning activities and about career exploration that can help you to select work that you will truly enjoy.

Let us elaborate on your using the power of the Brain Preference Test to guide your own life. Study Figure #25 on the page to the left. It shows a relationship between the quadrants of the test and sample career areas. For example the upper left quadrant involves logic, words, and numbers. If you scored high or dominant in this left-brain/abstract thinking area, you would be well advised to explore career paths that make use of logic, words, or numbers. Observers in business and industry have found that employees whose specific job descriptions make use of their specific brain preferences enjoy their work the most. Given the number of years you are most likely going to work, you are well advised to seek a career that you will really enjoy!

TABLE #5: SAMPLE CAREER AREAS RELATED TO QUADRANTS

UPPER LEFT, ABSTRACT QUADRANT D SCORE =	**UPPER RIGHT,ABSTRACT QUADRANT A SCORE =**
Focus on logic or words or math: Programmers Journalists Lawyers Scientists Technicians Accountants Science or math teachers	Focus on visualizing: System Analysts Theorists Planners Architects Entrepreneurs Artists Art teachers
LOWER LEFT, CONCRETE QUADRANT C SCORE =	**LOWER RIGHT, CONCRETE QUADRANT B SCORE =**
Focus on goals or directing: Administrators Directors Foremen Quarterbacks (See special discussion.)	Focus on doing or helping or teaming: Social workers Nurses Builders and fixers Sales people Athletes

FIGURE # 26

Now, record your scores on the preference test in the heading of each quadrant in TABLE #5 on the left page (or a copy of the table if you do not own this booklet). A score of 5 or 6 should lead you to explore career paths related to a quadrant. A score of 1 or 2 usually does not indicate strong preference matching. A score of 3 or 4 in a quadrant can be worth exploring depending on your scores in other quadrants. Later, I shall discuss an instance in which a person has strong score in all quadrants. Also, remember that no test is perfect; always pay attention to your personal feelings. High scores indicate areas worth exploring, not a mandate to restrict career exploration to just a high score area.

Use TABLE #5 with your preference test scores to consider carefully what general career areas you might best explore. The list in each quadrant is representative, not complete. Guidance counselors can help you to discover other career titles related to the brain characteristics of a particular quadrant.

Now let us look at some general information that applies to brains of all learners. First, look at the first basic suggestion in Figure #26 on the page to the left. You now know what learning styles and talents you prefer to use. **Whenever you are having difficulty learning or solving problems, try to switch to your preferred learning method or to your preferred thinking method.** These preferred methods are your learning and thinking strengths. School programs and teaching should provide you with choices in ways to learn and ways to demonstrate learning whenever possible. If they do not, this is something parents should encourage as needed improvement in school service.

Next, consider the second basic suggestion in Figure #26. These are times when there is no choice on learning style or on a talent that is needed for solving a specific problem. So, beginning now, **look for opportunities to improve any learning styles and grow any intelligences or talents that you now consider relative weaknesses.** Go to the activity lists for those items in Chapters 2 and 3 and practice doing the activities. When you grow your "whole brain" capabilities, you gain two powerful advantages. One, your multiple styles and talents will work together to make you more effective at learning and at solving specific problems. Two, your "whole brain" capabilities will enable you to do much better at adjusting to changing situations in your daily life. Indeed, it is worthwhile to develop you strengths in all quadrants even to the point where you might have high test scores in all quadrants. Then you have the talents to adjust to complex and changing situations. Consider an example. Pretend you are the quarterback of a team in the National Football League able to use such talents as these:

QUADRANT D LOGIC - - Look at the statistics. It is third down with one yard to go. We have a play that has gained three yards or more ninety percent of the time. I'll use it.

QUADRANT A VISUALIZATION - - I've been watching the other team for weaknesses. I close my eyes and picture a play that goes through the weak spot in their line. I'll use it.

QUADRANT B INTERPERSONAL APPEAL - - In the huddle, I say to the team "Fellows, we have got to make this touchdown for the sake of our coach and his job! Here is the play #9. Make it work!"

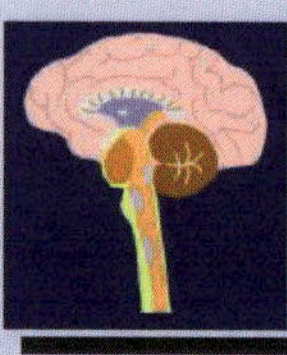

FIGURE # 27

Advice related to this rule of thumb is:

1. Use the rule when studying. At the end of your best attention span, switch to another activity for at least 5 or 10 minutes before returning to the studying.
2. The other activity can be a rest break, a short review session, a brief chat with someone, or even a little physical exercise.
3. This study-break-study or pulse approach will be far more effective than trying to learn without changing activity briefly. Also, avoid studying late at night when you should be getting a full night of rest. A full night of sleep is needed for best brain function, and the brain actually consolidates learning while you sleep.

QUADRANT C INTRAPERSONAL DIRECTION - - Center Jack has been losing yards with false starts. You say "Jack, no false start this time. Get it right or you'll be out of the game!"

Can you also imagine how having strong talents in each quadrant could help you if you were the head of a large and complex company? You would have to deal with accountants (quadrant D), visualizing or predicting the future of products (quadrant A), supporting and motivating your employees (quadrant B), and correcting or directing any poor performer (quadrant C). In other words, developing multiple intelligences or talents increases your personal management power.

Now, consider the rule of thumb in Figure #27 to the left. Observations have shown that **a person's best attention span roughly equals his or age plus two minutes up to a maximum of about thirty minutes.** So, if you are fifteen, you probably find it difficult to just listen to a lecture for over fifteen to twenty minutes unless the lecture is interrupted with discussion or some other activity. While you cannot control teachers who ignore such important information, you can control the way you study or do homework on your own time. Follow the advice below Figure #27. A little more elaboration on this time advice can be useful.

Figure #28 below shows a second reason for alternating or switching activities.

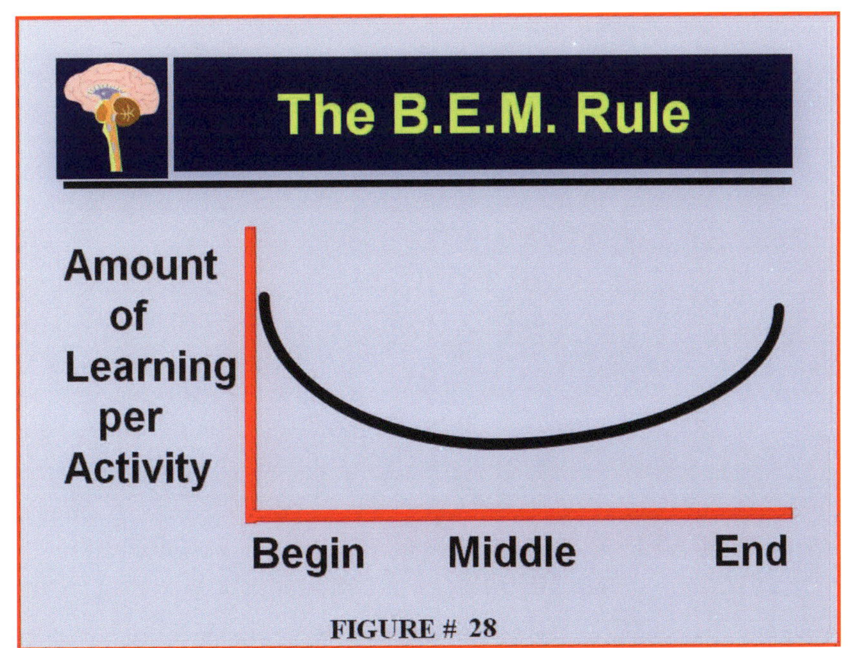

FIGURE # 28

Observations have shown that, for any <u>one</u> activity, maximum learning occurs at the beginning and the end of the activity. Less learning occurs in the middle of the learning activity. This Beginning-End-Middle or B.E.M. rule is important. So, if you try to read or to study for a test for one hour straight, you are making a mistake because the middle time of this relatively long activity is too long and inefficient. What works better is to study or read in fifteen minute blocks with a change or "break" in between. Again, the break can be almost any other activity such as going to another room and splashing water on your fact, having somebody ask you a question on what you just read, drawing and writing some review notes, or even just closing your eyes

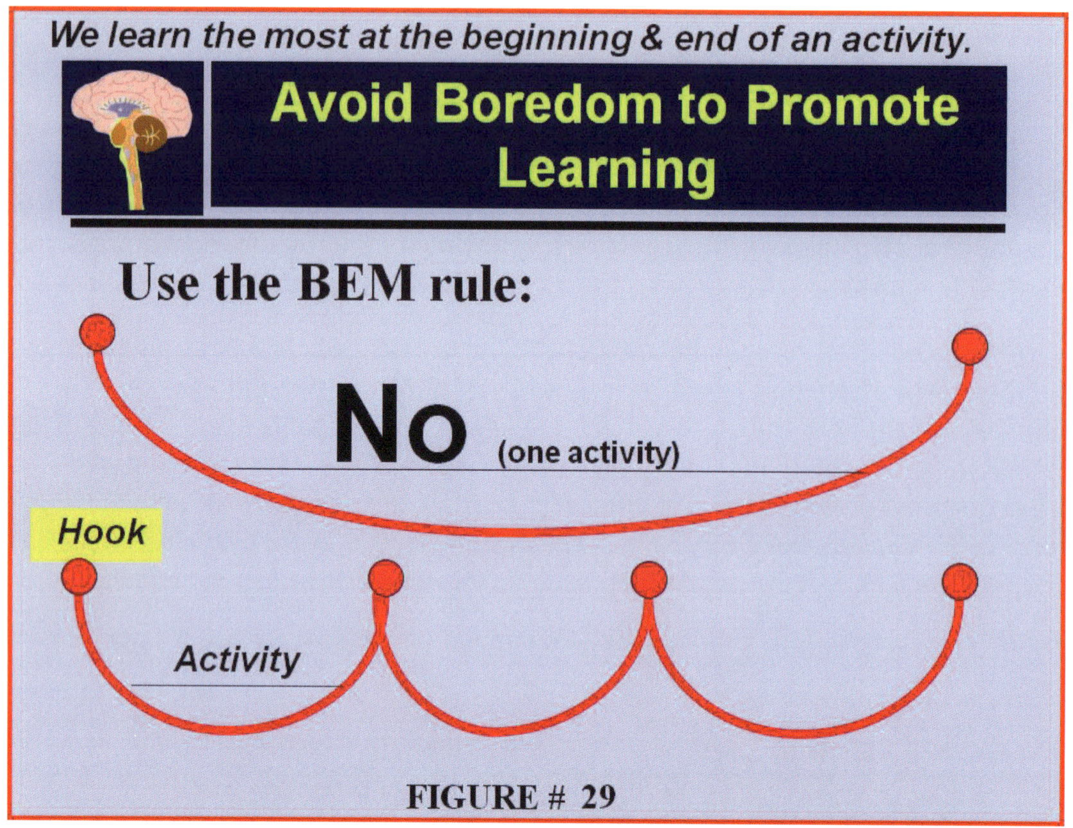

FIGURE # 29

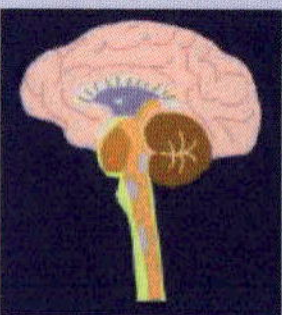

Brain Reality: Memory Can Be Helped in Specific Ways

- Repetition
- Experience "episodes"
- Procedural practice
- Emotional context
- Downtime followed by timely review or application

FIGURE # 30

and relaxing for a minute or two. The important point is you are switching activities and keeping your middle time shorter.

Figure #29 on the left page is a picture that will help you to remember to use the B.E.M. rule that avoids long, boring middles. Try to avoid any long boring study sessions like that portrayed by the top curve. Instead study in pulse sessions with short breaks or changed activities between sessions as shown by the bottom lines. Incidentally, the small HOOK label at the start of the pulse sessions is another piece of advice. It is there to remind you to think about the real life value of materials you are going to study before you start your study session. That helps to "hook" you to appreciating the value of the learning you are about to pursue.

Our last Figure #30 to the left contains some parting general advice on remembering what you learn. Again, the advice applies to everyone. Here is a review of the suggestions in Figure #30 for remembering what you learn:

a. **Repetition.** - - After a short learning session, list or map and then review the main points learned. Repeat them to yourself.

b. **Experience "episodes."** - - Arrange some experience, experiment, or event about what you have learned. If you do something that reinforces the learning, this helps the brain to remember. For example, the simple action of drawing a picture of what you learned will help fix it in your memory.

c. **Procedural practice.** - - If what you learned is a procedure or a set of steps on how to do something, practice it several times. This is repetition that aids memory again. However, practicing the steps helps much more than just trying to memorize a description of the steps.

d. **Emotional context.** - - If you can relate your learning to some emotional event in your life or to a visual image about which you have strong feelings, you will remember it better. Find such connections whenever possible.

e. **Downtime followed by timely review or application.** - - After learning something, move away from it for a while. Then return and review or use the information a day later and even a week later. This helps build lasting memories of what you have learned. Spaced review or repetition and practice are powerful tools.

All of the techniques fit with the learn, change activity, return to learning sequence we reviewed in relation to Figure #29 and pulse learning. Use these techniques along with what you have learned about how your brain works best and you can become a powerful learner.

<u>Personal Review Questions</u>

1. In what quadrant did you score highest in the brain preference test? Circle one (or more if some quadrant scores were tied):

left-abstract	right-abstract
left-concrete	right-concrete

TABLE 6: SUMMARY OF MAIN POINTS EXPLAINED IN THIS HANDBOOK

1. Using brain-friendly techniques improves learning.
2. LEARNING HOW TO LEARN is an important subject.
3. Brain characteristics vary based on left-right dominance and upper-lower thinking preferences.
4. The left brain favors logic, words, and numbers.
5. The right brain favors randomness and images. (Use drawings in your notes.)
6. Different styles of receiving information include auditory, visual, somatic, and reflective.
7. Use your preferred style for difficult learning, but grow your comfort with other styles also.
8. Graphic organizers can be useful to most learners.
9. The brain tends to remember useful information.
10. Using multiple senses usually results in more learning than using one sense.
11. Discussion with others can aid learning.
12. Using information gives it meaning and helps learning.
13. Teaching others helps you to learn more.
14. Each of us has multiple types of intelligence or thinking techniques, but most of us have intelligence or talent preferences.
15. As with learning styles, use your preferred intelligences but grow others also to gain the most thinking power.
16. Emotional intelligence is especially important to career success.
17. A cause and effect diagram can be a powerful thinking and planning tool. Use it to grow planning power in your pre-frontal lobes.
18. A Brain Preference Test can give you important information on your thinking preferences.
19. Matching your thinking preferences to a career area can help you to enjoy your work.
20. Be conscious of your best attention span (age + 2 minutes to a maximum of 30).
21. Use the beginning-end-middle or B.E.M. rule to improve learning efficiency. Alternate study with short breaks or changed activity.
22. Repetition aids remembering.
23. Experience or doing something with what you have learned aids remembering.
24. Experiencing emotion with learning promotes remembering.
25. Downtime (breaks, rest, or sleep) after learning and then review or using the information promotes remembering.

2. Does the test result above seem to match your earlier analyses of your left-right and talent tendencies? Circle one:

yes no

3. If "no" in #2 above, describe any differences.

4. Based on your use of this booklet, describe three changes you have made or plan to make in the way you study.

   a.

   b.

   c.

NOTE: Answers represent your personal data and thus are not in the Appendix.

TABLE #6 ON PAGE 39 TO THE LEFT SUMMARIZES THE MAIN POINTS CONTAINED IN THIS BOOKLET. USE IT TO REVIEW AND/OR TO GO BACK TO THE TABLE OF CONTENTS FOR ANY TOPIC YOU NEED TO VISIT AGAIN. I WISH YOU THE BEST IN YOUR BRAIN-FRIENDLY LEARNING.

Appendix

Answers to Review Questions

Review Questions for Chapter 1

All four statements are true.

Review Questions for Chapter 2

1. R
2. L
3. S
4. L
5. R

Review Questions for Chapter 3

1. b, process or use information
2. Intrapersonal intelligence
3. Two
4. Emotional intelligence
5. Cause & effect chart

Index

CPSIA information can be obtained
at www.ICGtesting.com
229179LV00006B

* 9 7 8 1 6 0 8 4 4 2 9 8 0 *